CEDAR CREST COLLEGE LIBRARY
ALLENTOWN, PA

BACH

Cantata No. 140

The Score of the New Bach Edition

Backgrounds · Analysis

Views and Comments

NORTON CRITICAL SCORES

Johann Sebastian Bach

CANTATA NO. 140
Wachet auf, ruft uns die Stimme

The Score of the New Bach Edition

Backgrounds · Analysis

Views and Comments

Edited by

GERHARD HERZ
UNIVERSITY OF LOUISVILLE

721200

W · W · NORTON & COMPANY · INC · *New York*

Copyright © 1972 by W. W. Norton & Company, Inc.

Published simultaneously in Canada
by George J. McLeod, Limited, Toronto.

FIRST EDITION

Library of Congress Catalog Card No. 79-139396

SBN 393 02154 8 CLOTH EDITION
SBN 393 09555 X PAPER EDITION

PRINTED IN THE UNITED STATES OF AMERICA

1 2 3 4 5 6 7 8 9 0

Contents

Contents

Preface

The introductory chapter in the present editor's Norton Critical Score of Bach's Cantata No. 4 (New York, 1967) summarized the history of the cantata as a genre, its place in the Lutheran service of Bach's time, and the fate of Bach's cantatas after his death. Rather than reprint the same historical essay as a preface to Cantata No. 140, the revolutionary new chronology of Bach's vocal music is presented here for the first time in English.[1] This chronology is the result of painstaking labor on the part of a number of Bach scholars who, in 1950, the bicentennial of Bach's death, decided to prepare a new critical edition of Bach's works.[2]

The B-minor Mass, edited by Friedrich Smend, was one of the first volumes of the *NBA*; the score appeared in 1954, Smend's critical commentary two years later. Both still accepted the old chronology that Philipp Spitta had established in 1880.[3] It was Smend's great misfortune that, in the years during which he completed his exhaustive work on the B-minor Mass, Alfred Dürr and Georg von Dadelsen made definitive and philologically convincing discoveries regarding the dates of Bach's compositions in general and of his Leipzig vocal music in particular. They combined two different yet equally valid research methods: a systematic analysis of the paper and watermarks of all Bach manuscripts[4] and an investigation of Bach's handwriting, that of his family,[5] and that

1. Vernon Gotwals, *Bach's Church Cantatas Dated: An Interim Report*, in *Notes*, XXI/3 (Summer 1964) , 340-49, did not present Bach's vocal output in sequence.
2. *Neue Bach Ausgabe* (hereinafter abbreviated *NBA*) , edited by the Johann-Sebastian-Bach-Institut, Göttingen, and the Bach-Archiv, Leipzig; Kassel, etc., 1954 ff.
3. *Johann Sebastian Bach*, 2 vols., Leipzig, 1873 and 1880; English translation by Clara Bell and J. A. Fuller-Maitland, 1889, reprinted 1951.
4. Alfred Dürr, *Zur Chronologie der Leipziger Vokalwerke J. S. Bachs*, in *Bach-Jahrbuch*, XLIV (1957) , 5-162.
5. Georg von Dadelsen, *Bemerkungen zur Handschrift Johann Sebastian Bachs, seiner Familie und seines Kreises* (Tübinger Bach-Studien, 1) , Trossingen, 1957.

of his principal copyists.[6] Information deduced by one technique supported and reinforced evidence from the other. Starting with the few specifically dated compositions, and using the calendar of the Leipzig church year as a background on which to project these data, Dürr and von Dadelsen eventually arrived at a startling new chronology. It supersedes that of Spitta, which had remained unshaken until the late 1950s.

I am deeply grateful to Dr. Dürr and Professor von Dadelsen for their kind and selfless permission to make full use of their findings for the chronology presented here. For the final organization of the material,[7] and for changes and additions—particularly of compositions that have not come down to us in primary sources—I must take full responsibility. The desire to include a maximum of information in a minimum of space resulted eventually in a chart that owes additional information to a third prominent German Bach scholar, Professor Werner Neumann.[8] The column on the sources of Bach's texts further incorporates some of the findings of Ferdinand Zander[9] as well as the recent revelation of G. C. Lehms as author of ten cantata texts,[10] to which Dr. Dürr first drew my attention. To all of them I want to express my sincere appreciation.

With the acceptance of the new chronology, which necessitates the re-dating of two-thirds of Bach's cantatas alone, a whole world of conjectures and interpretations by Spitta and his countless followers[11] collapses and a new image of Bach emerges.[12] It is hoped that this new and more accurate dating of Bach's compositions may serve to promote a better understanding of the evolution of Bach's style and shed new light on his personality.

GERHARD HERZ

6. Dürr, *op. cit.*, and von Dadelsen, *Beiträge zur Chronologie der Werke Johann Sebastian Bachs* (Tübinger Bach-Studien, 4/5), Trossingen, 1958. Both studies used as an indispensable tool Wisso Weiss's stupendous catalogue of the paper and watermarks of all the original manuscripts by Bach: *Papier und Wasserzeichen der Notenhandschriften von Johann Sebastian Bach*, unpublished; since 1955, typed copies have been available to the editors of the *NBA* at Göttingen, Leipzig, Princeton, N. J., etc.

7. In its first stage it resembled von Dadelsen's Chart A; cf. von Dadelsen, *Beiträge*, pp. 123-33.

8. *Johann Sebastian Bach—Sämtliche Kantatentexte*, Leipzig, 1956; and *Handbuch der Kantaten Johann Sebastian Bachs*, 3rd ed., Leipzig, 1967.

9. *Die Dichter der Kantatentexte Johann Sebastian Bachs*, dissertation, Cologne, 1967.

10. Elisabeth Noack, *Georg Christian Lehms, ein Textdichter Johann Sebastian Bachs*, in *Bach-Jahrbuch*, 1970, pp. 7-18.

11. Friedrich Smend still belongs among them; cf. F. Smend, *Was bleibt?*, in *Der Kirchenmusiker*, XIII (1962), 1 ff.

12. But it will hardly be Friedrich Blume's overdrawn *Outlines of a New Picture of Bach*, in *Music and Letters*, XLIV (1963), 214-27.

HISTORICAL
BACKGROUND

The New Chronology of Bach's Vocal Music

Explanations and Abbreviations

GENERAL

AMB Notebook *Klavierbüchlein für Anna Magdalena Bach*
aut. autograph
B. J. S. Bach
B-Mass B-minor Mass
Brandenb. Conc. Brandenburg Concerto(s)
c. century
ca. circa
cant. cantata
chor. chorale
Cö. Cöthen
congrat. congratulatory
cont. continuo
cop. copyist
East. Or. Easter Oratorio
enlarg. enlargement
ext. extant
fragm. fragment
Lp. Leipzig

Mühlh. Mühlhausen
org. organ
orig. origin or original
parod. parody, parodies or parodied
pr. printed
Probestück trial composition by which the candidate for a vacant position demonstrates his qualifications
pt. performing part
rec. recitative
reperf. re-performance or re-performed
rev. revision or revised
sc. score
sec. secular
t.p. title page
Univ. University
Wei. Weimar
Xmas Or. Christmas Oratorio (its six parts—cantatas—are indicated by Roman numbers I through VI)

I

Column I gives the date of the *performance*, not of the *creation* of the composition. However, in the majority of cases, Bach, the greatest composer of sacred *Gebrauchsmusik*, wrote his cantatas only when time and occasion demanded. As is not the case with Beethoven, for example, Bach's dates of composition and of *first* performance lie close together. The many cantatas that have come down to us in composing scores—i.e., not in later revisions or fair copies—show by their handwriting the extreme pressure under which Bach labored to ready the composition for rehearsal and performance. There are documented cases where only one day remained between completion of the score and performance. On the other hand, the reader must be warned that sometimes the first *datable* performance does not coincide with the true first performance. For example, Cantata 4 may well have been composed for Easter 1707, as Bach's *Probestück* (trial composition) for the Mühlhausen position. The parts by which the composition survives are, however, demonstrably from 1724; hence the first performance of *Christ lag in Todesbanden* that can actually be documented falls on Easter 1724. However, cases such as this are in the minority.

Only when the new edition of Bach's works is completed shall we know the exact relationship between time of composition and first datable performance. From what is known to date, one may assume that for the vast majority of Bach's cantatas the dates of composition and of first provable performance will remain close neighbors.

II

Column II, *Occasion*, specifies the particular Sunday, holiday or other churchly, secular, civic, or private event for which the work was written.[1]

Abbreviations (other than self-explanatory ones) :

1 [, 2, 3, etc.] p. Trin. 1st [, 2nd, 3rd, etc.] Sunday after Trinity
2 p. Epiph. 2nd Sunday after Epiphany
Annivers. anniversary
B'day birthday
Consecr. consecration
Coron. coronation
Epiph. Epiphany

Fun. Serv. Funeral Service
Inaug. inauguration
Mem. Serv. Memorial Service
p. after
Sun. Sunday
Trin. Trinity
Whits. Whitsuntide (Pentecost)
Xmas Christmas

III

Column III, *BWV*, gives the number of the work in *Bach-Werke-Verzeichnis*, the thematic catalogue of Bach's works compiled by Wolfgang Schmieder in 1950. Schmieder's numbers have no chronological significance, but merely follow the order in which the cantatas were published by the Bach Gesellschaft in the 19th century. In this column the following symbols and abbreviations are used:

BWV numbers enclosed in **parentheses** imply that this is not the first performance but a re-performance (and frequently also a revision) of this particular composition.
Numbers following a **diagonal slash (/)** after the BWV number indicate specific movements of this composition.

1. For a full account of the Lutheran church calendar, the reader is referred to Charles Sanford Terry, *Joh. Seb. Bach, Cantata Texts, Sacred and Secular (With a Reconstruction of the Leipzig Liturgy of His Period)* , London, 1926; reprinted London, 1964.

The small letter **a** after the BWV number usually signifies the first version (*Urform*) of that work.

App. Appendix (Anhang) refers to Schmieder's category of lost compositions, of which the text or some other documentary evidence has survived.

Roman numerals indicate that the work is not included in the Appendix of Schmieder's BWV. The work can, however, be found under this number in Werner Neumann, *Handbuch der Kantaten*, p. 242 ff.

V

Column V, *Text*, summarizes the text sources. The primary poet is listed first; arabic numerals indicate individual movements drawn from other text sources.

Abbreviations:

NT New Testament
OT Old Testament
par. paraphrase or paraphrased (usually referring to hymn verses)

Ps. Psalm (s)
v. verse (or stanza) of a hymn

Text authors whose names appear in abbreviated form:

ÄJvS-R Ämilie Juliane von Schwarzburg-Rudolstadt
AvB Margrave Albrecht von Brandenburg

MvZ Mariane von Ziegler
Pic. Christian Friedrich Henrici, whose pen name was Picander
Weiss Christian Weiss, Sr.

VI

Column VI, *Mvts.* (Movements), lists:

on **line 1:** the total number of movements in the composition;
on **line 2:** the number of choral movements, except for those appearing
on **line 3:** Here the number of simple four-part chorale harmonizations is given. An * after the number on the third line implies that the instruments do not go *colla parte* but play a more or less independent role. (*) indicates that only one or two instruments play obbligato parts.
A number enclosed in **parentheses** signifies solo rather than choral execution. In spite of the observations by Wilhelm Rust (editor of most of the cantata volumes in the old *Bach-Gesellschaft* edition), Arnold Schering, and, more recently, Wilhelm Ehmann, the authorities are by no means agreed on the question of solo versus choral execution (see footnote to Cantata 4, p. 21). In six cantatas (Nos. 71, 21, 76, 24, 110 and 195) Bach specified solo treatment in certain movements, thereby establishing criteria by which the present-day performer may decide when solo execution or reduced vocal forces seem to be required. Robert Shaw's recent recording of the B-minor Mass is a splendid example of the application of the solo-tutti principle.

In the chart, where so much detail is compressed into such limited space, the author has attempted to use parentheses to qualify what might otherwise appear too categorical, as if to say: it is not quite as simple as it seems (cf. footnotes to Cantatas 132, 59, 4, etc. on pages 12, 15, 21, etc.)

id. identical. This usually means the two chorales that close parts I and II of a two-part cantata are musically identical.

The movements of cantatas in two parts are listed as follows: (e.g.) 11:6+5

A listing such as: 4 or

       2 1+

       0 1*

leaves it to the reader whether to assign a chorale richly embellished by obbligato instruments to the second line (reserved for choruses) or to the third (on which chorale harmonizations are listed). The question of when a richly adorned chorale becomes a simple chorale fantasy is thus left open.

VII and VIII

Columns VII and VIII show not only whether the autograph score and the original performing parts have survived but also the present location of these manuscripts.

Column VII, *Score*, gives the whereabouts of the autograph scores; column VIII, *Pts. & Cop.*, that of the original performing parts. The line or lines below identify the principal copyist(s) of these parts.

Brackets indicate that a set of parts, or even the score, is incomplete.

Location symbols:

Bruss. Brussels
Cambr. Cambridge, England
Cob. Coburg
Copenh. Copenhagen (Royal Library)
Cö. Cöthen
Darm. Darmstadt
disp. dispersed
Dresd. Dresden
E.Bn. East Berlin (Deutsche Staatsbibliothek)
LC Library of Congress, Washington, D.C.
Ln. London
Lp. Leipzig (Bach-Archiv, which now houses the precious holdings of the St. Thomas's School Library)

NA not accessible
N.Y. New York
NYML Morgan Library, New York City
NYPL New York Public Library
Paris Paris (Conservatoire de Musique)
Pr. in private possession (followed by a geographical indication, where known)
Switz. Switzerland
U.S.A. United States of America
W.Bn. West Berlin (Staatsbibliothek, Preussischer Kulturbesitz)
W. Germ. West Germany

Abbreviations for Copyists:

The principal copyists whose handwritings are to be found in the performing parts of Bach's Leipzig vocal music are primarily members of his family and, above all, his pupils. The following have been identified by name:

AM Anna Magdalena Bach (1701–60)

CPE Carl Philipp Emanuel Bach (1714–88)

GHB Gottfried Heinrich Bach (1724–63)

JBB Johann Bernhard Bach (1700–43), a cousin of J. S. Bach

JCF Johann Christoph Friedrich Bach (1732–95)

JSB Johann Sebastian Bach (i.e. autograph)

Kr. Johann Ludwig Krebs, Bach's favorite pupil

K Johann Andreas Kuhnau, nephew (?) of Bach's predecessor as cantor of St. Thomas, served as principal copyist from February 7, 1723 through December 30, 1725. Subscripts indicate the stages of development in Kuhnau's handwriting: K_1, the early period, K_2, the middle period, K_3, a transitional stage from middle to late forms, and K_4, the final phase.

M Christian Gottlob Meissner

WF Wilhelm Friedemann Bach (1710–84)

Other copyists are represented in the recent literature by symbols. The **major copyists** are signified by capital letters; before identification, Kuhnau was known as "Principal Copyist A," and Meissner as "Principal Copyist B." Copyist C served Bach simultaneously with Kuhnau and Meissner; D,E,F,G, and H represent the chief copyists from 1729 to the last years of their master's life.

Minor copyists bear such numbers as Ih, IIa or IIf, the Roman numerals indicating the Leipzig *Jahrgang*[2] during which this copyist first appears. The Roman numeral V applies to copyists who served Bach in the 1730s and 1740s.

IX

Column IX, *Wm.*, lists the principal watermark(s) of the paper on which the score and/or the parts of the composition were written.

Abbreviations of watermarks that consist of more than initials and are not self-explanatory:

D.Eag. Double Eagle

GAW GAW + (usually) Posthorn

) Halfmoon, the chief watermark of Leipzig *Jahrgang* II

Horn Posthorn

IAI Stag +IAI

ICF Crowned figure between branches above ICF

IMK IMK + small halfmoon, the principal watermark of Leipzig *Jahrgang* I

ma MA watermark, small size

MA MA watermark, medium size

MA MA watermark, large size

Ornam. Baroque Ornament

S.CoA Schönburg Coat of Arms

Sw.I, Sw.II two different watermarks showing crossed swords

SW Chalice + SW

2. *Jahrgang* is a one-year cycle of church compositions. Since Bach entered upon his Leipzig duties on May 30, 1723, his first Leipzig *Jahrgang* begins with the Sunday after Trinity.

Four different watermarks show the heraldic Coat of Arms of Zedwitz. They are abbreviated as follows:

Z.I Zedwitz Coat of Arms only

Z.II Zedwitz Coat of Arms + monogram

Z+IWI Zedwitz Coat of Arms + IWI

Z+NM Zedwitz Coat of Arms + NM

ZVM Crown and Posthorn + letters: ZVMILIKAV

X

This column, *Remarks*, lists historical peculiarities or special characteristics that distinguish the work in question. It may show that the composition is a solo cantata. The abbreviation "solo cant." appearing between parentheses **(solo cant.)** indicates that the chorus is used only in the concluding chorale. More frequently, the column shows the first performance in relation to later, often revised, performances. Above all, it lists Bach's frequent self-borrowings, those adaptations or "parodies" that increase dramatically with the passing of time.

XI

Column XI, *Old Date*, shows the former dating as it still appears in Schmieder's catalogue, BWV, of 1950 and in its third unchanged edition of 1961. The discrepancies are particularly glaring in the works of Bach's second year in Leipzig, i.e., from 6/11/1724 to 5/27/1725.

MUHLHAUSEN AND WEIMAR CANTATAS

I Date	II Occasion	III BWV	IV Title	V Text	VI Mvts.	VII Score	VIII Pts. & Cop.	IX Wm.	X Remarks	XI Old Date
1707										
4/24	Easter	4?	Christ lag in Todesbanden	Luther 1524			See 4/9/1724		Probestück for Mühlhausen ?	1724 (or Wei.?)
Summer	Memorial of 5/30 fire ?	131	Aus der Tiefe rufe ich, Herr, zu dir	Ps. 130 + Ringwaldt 1588	5 3 0	Pr. N.Y.		CB¹ + Eagle	Aut. postscript: "Org(anista) Molhusin(o?)"	1707
Aug. ?	Mourning service for B's uncle, Tobias Lämmerhirt?¹ᵃ	106	Gottes Zeit ist die allerbeste Zeit	OT; NT; Luther 1524; Reusner 1533	7? 3? 0				Copy (sc.) by Penzel, Lp., 1768	1711?
1708										
2/4	Inaug. of new Town Council	71	Gott ist mein König	OT; Heermann 1630; Eilmar ?	7 4 0	E.Bn.	E.Bn. JSB	CB + Eagle	Aut. date (on sc.)²	1708
6/5	Wedding: aunt of B's bride/J.L. Stauber?	196	Der Herr denket an uns	Ps. 115	5 2 0				Copy (sc.) from Kirnberger's estate	1708
?	?	223	Meine Seele soll Gott loben						Incomplete³ (a duet only?)	

1. Watermarks frequently show the initial letters of the owner of the paper mill or the paper marker; in this case, those of Christoph Becker of Mühlhausen (ca. 1672-1707).

1a. Hermann Schmalfuss in *Bach-Jahrbuch*, 1970, p. 40 f., presents fresh evidence that might well connect Cantata 106 with the funeral service on June 3, 1708, for the only surviving sister of Bach's Mühlhausen friend and theological mentor, Pastor G. C. Eilmar: Dorothea Susanna Tilesius, who died at the early age of 34. The earlier date (August 1707) makes, however, more sense from a stylistic point of view.

2. Only extant cantata by Bach printed during his lifetime (1708).

3. Copy, once owned by Spitta, is now lost. Cf. Philipp Spitta, *Johann Sebastian Bach*, 3 vols., New York (and London), 1951 (reprinted from the English edition of 1889), I, p. 343 f.

I Date	II Occasion	III BWV	IV Title	V Text	VI Mvts.	VII Score	VIII Pts. & Cop.	IX Wm.	X Remarks	XI Old Date
1709 Feb.	Inaug. of new Town Council	XXIV	[Music and text lost]						record of payment to JSB ext.: 2/7/1709	
1708-10	?	150	Nach dir, Herr, verlanget mich	Ps. 25 + unknown poet	7 4 0				Copy (sc.) by Penzel, Lp., 1753	bef. 1712
1713										
2/19	Sexagesima	18?	Gleichwie der Regen und Schnee vom Himmel fällt	Neumeister; 2: OT; 5: Spengler 1524	5 or 0 1 1		E.Bn. mostly JSB	AA⁴	or 2/4/1714	1713 or 1714
2/23?	B'day: Duke of Saxe-Weissenfels	208	Was mir behagt ist nur die muntre Jagd!	Salomo Franck	15 (2) 0	E.Bn.		IHS⁴	B's 1st sec. cant. (Solo cant.):S,A,T,B. Mvts. 7,15,13 parod. in BWV 68, 149 & V⁵	1716
12/10	2. Advent [on t.p. (top): "per ogni tempo"]	either 21	Ich hatte viel Bekümmernis	Franck ?; Ps.; NT; Neumark 1657	11:6+5 4 0		E.Bn. 1st set: JSB	MK⁴	Probestück for Zachow's post at Halle?	1714
		or 63	Christen ätzet diesen Tag	Heineccius ?	7 2 0		W.Bn. 9 pts: JSB	AA	As above, but BWV 21 is more credible	1723
1714										
3/25	Palm Sunday	182	Himmelskönig sei willkommen	Franck ?; 2: Ps.; 7: Stockmann 1633	8 3 0	W.Bn.	E.Bn.	Sc:W⁴ +AA; some pts: MK	Cf. 3/25/1724	1714 or 1715
3/30?	Good Friday		Reinhard Keiser's Mark Passion				E.Bn.	9 pts: MK	Cf. 4/19/1726	
4/22	Jubilate	12	Weinen, Klagen, Sorgen, Zagen	Franck ?; 7: Rodigast 1674	7 1 1	W.Bn.	W.Bn. 5 pts: JSB	Sc:AA	Cf. 4/30/1724 Parod. 2: BWV 232; 7: BWV 69a	1714?

10

Date	Occasion	BWV	Title	Text source	Nos.	Source	Misc.	Notes	Year
5/20	Whits.	172	Erschallet, ihr Lieder, erklinget, ihr Saiten!	Franck ?; 2: NT; 6: Nicolai 1599	6⁸ 1 1(*)	E.Bn. partly JSB	7 pts: AA; 2: IMK	Cf. 5/28/1724	1724 or 1725
6/17	"3 post Trinit" on t.p. (bottom)[7]	(21)						Re-performance for departure from Weimar of the critically ill 18-year-old Prince Johann Ernst of Saxe-Weimar (d. 8/1/1715.)	
7/15	7 p. Trin.	54?	Widerstehe doch der Sünde	J. C. Lehms	3 0 0	Copy by J. G. Walther (Bruss.)		Solo cant: A. 1: parod. in BWV 247/53	ca. 1730
8/12	11 p. Trin.	199	Mein Herze schwimmt im Blut	Lehms; 6: Heermann 1630	8 0 0	Copenh [W.Bn.] mostly: JSB	8 pts: MK	Solo cant: S. cf. 8/8/1723	1714 or 1715
12/2	1. Advent	61	Nun komm, der Heiden Heiland I	Neumeister; 1: Luther 1524; 4: NT; 6: Nicolai 1599	6 or 2 1+ 0 1*	E.Bn.	IHS	Aut. date cf. 11/28/1723	1714
12/30	Sun. p. Xmas	152	Tritt auf die Glaubensbahn	Franck 1715	6 0 0	E.Bn.	IHS	Solo cant: S, B	1715
1715									
1/27	3 p. Epiph.	72?	Alles nur nach Gottes Willen	Franck 1715; 6: AvB 1547	6 1 1	E.Bn. W.Bn.		Cf. 1/27/1726 Urform of Wei. orig.? 1: parod. in BWV 235	1723-25 (or Cö. or Wei.?)
2/24	Sexagesima	(18)?						Cf. 2/19/1713	
3/24	Oculi	80a	Alles was von Gott geboren	Franck 1715; 6: Luther 1529	6 0 1			Urform of "Ein feste Burg . . .," cf. 10/31/1724(?)	1716

II

4. Weimar watermarks.
5. Lost cantata for inauguration of Town Council on 8/29/1740.
6. In the Leipzig version (in D major) the opening chorus is to be repeated.
7. Cf. 12/10/1713 above]

I Date	II Occasion	III BWV	IV Title	V Text	VI Mvts.	VII Score	VIII Pts. & Cop.	IX Wm.	X Remarks	XI Old Date
1715 (cont.)										
4/21	Easter	31	*Der Himmel lacht! die Erde jubilieret*	Franck 1715; 9: N. Herman 1575	9 / 1 / 1*		NA mostly: JSB	?	Cf. 4/9/1724	1715 rev. 1731
6/16	Trin.	165	*O heil'ges Geist- und Wasserbad*	Franck 1715; 6: Helmbold 1575	6 / 0 / 1				(Solo cant.): S, A, T,B; cf. 6/4/1724	1724?
7/14	4. p. Trin.	185	*Barmherziges Herze der ewigen Liebe*	Franck 1715; 6: Agricola 1529	6 / 1 / 1(*)	W.Bn. E.Bn.	mostly: JSB	Sc: W 11 pts: AA	(Solo cant.): S, A, T,B; cf. 6/20/1723	1715
[Death of Prince Johann Ernst causes a 2-months mourning period from 8/4 (7 p. Trin.) through 9/22 (14 p. Trin.).]										
10/6	16 p. Trin.	161	*Komm, du süsse Todesstunde*	Franck 1715; 6: Knoll 1605	6 / 1 / 1(*)				survives in 3 18th c. copies	1715
11/3	20 p. Trin.	162	*Ach! ich sehe, jetzt, da ich zur Hochzeit gehe*	Franck 1715; 6: Rosenmüller 1652	6 / 0 / 1	W.Bn.	W.Bn. mostly: JSB	mostly: AA	(Solo cant.): S,A,T,B Cf. 10/10/1723	1715
11/24	23 p. Trin.	163	*Nur jedem das Seine*	Franck 1715; 6: Heermann 1630	6 / 0 / 1	W.Bn.		MK	(Solo cant.): S,A,T,B	1715
12/22	4. Advent	132	*Bereitet die Wege, bereitet die Bahn!*	Franck 1715; 6: Kreuziger 1524	6 / 0 / (1)8	W.Bn.	[W.Bn.] 1 pt.	Sc:MK pt:AA	Aut. date (Solo cant.): S,A,T,B 6 = BWV 164/6?	1715
1716										
1/19	2 p. Epiph.	155	*Mein Gott, wie lang, ach lange*	Franck 1715; 5: Speratus 1524	5 / 0 / 1	E.Bn.		MK	(Solo cant.); S,A,T,B	1716
4/19	B'day: Prince Ernst August of Saxe-Weimar	(208)		Revision and re-performance: Cf. 2/23/1713!						

Date	Occasion	BWV	Title	Text source	Nos.			Notes	Year
12/6	2. Advent	70a	*Wachet! betet! betet! wachet!*	Franck 1717; 6: Keymann 1658	6 1 1*	W.Bn. 3 pts: JSB	3 pts: AA	Cf. 11/21/1723 BWV 70 adds 4 rec. + 1 chor.	1716
12/13	3. Advent	186a	*Ärgre dich, o Seele, nicht*	Franck 1717; 6: Helmbold 1563	6 1 1*(?)	W.Bn. (not aut.)		Cf. 7/11/1723 BWV 186 adds 4 rec. + 1 chor.	1716
12/20	4. Advent	147a	*Herz und Mund und Tat und Leben*	Franck 1717; 6: Kolrose ca. 1535	6 1 1°	W.Bn. W.Bn. (both of Lp. origin)	Sc: partly MK	BWV 147: additions as above. Cf. 7/2/1723	1716
				CÖTHEN CANTATAS					
1718									
12/10	B'day: Prince Leopold	66a	*Der Himmel dacht auf Anhalts Ruhm und Glück*	Hunold	8 1 0			Urform of BWV 66 Cf. 4/10/1724	1718
		App. 5?	*Lobet den Herrn, alle seine Heerscharen*	Hunold; 1: Ps. 103	7 1 0			Only text ext.	
1719									
1/1	New Year	134a	*Die Zeit, die Tag und Jahre macht*	Hunold	8 1 0	[Paris] E.Bn. JSB?	"Wild Man" (= Cö.)	Urform of BWV 134 Cf. 4/11/1724	1718-19
1720									
1/1	New Year	App. 6?	*Dich loben die lieblichen Strahlen der Sonne*	Hunold	5 0 0			Only text ext.	
Before 11/23	Hamburg Probestück?	(21)?						See 12/10/1713; a second set of parts on Cö. paper by Cö. copyist suggests a performance, in d minor (Kammerton), with all soli sung by Soprano, in Mattheson's presence (?), at Jakobi Kirche.	

8. Final chorale is missing in Bach's score but extant in Franck's text.

9. The music of the last movement (chorale) is lost.

I Date	II Occasion	III BWV	IV Title	V Text	VI Mvts.	VII Score	VIII Pts. & Cop.	IX Wm.	X Remarks	XI Old Date
1720 (cont.)										
12/10	Leopold's birthday	App. 7	Heut ist gewiss ein guter Tag	Hunold	10 1? 0				Only text ext.	
1722?										
7/29	B'day: Prince of Anhalt-Zerbst	XXII								
12/10	Leopold's birthday	173a?	Durchlauchtster Leopold	? (Hunold died 8/6/1721)	8 0 0	E.Bn.		"Wild Man"	Urform of BWV 173 Cf. 5/29/1724	1717
1723?										
1/1	New Year	184a?	Erwünschtes Freudenlicht	?	6 0 0				Id. with App. 8? Urform of BWV 184. Cf. 5/30/1724	Cö. period?

The following cantatas and cantata movements may also be of Cöthen origin:

I Date	II Occasion	III BWV	IV Title	V Text	VI Mvts.	VII Score	VIII Pts. & Cop.	IX Wm.	X Remarks	XI Old Date
1717—1723										
	Wedding	202	Weichet nur betrübte Schatten	?	9 0 0				Solo cant: S. Only 1730 copy of sc. ext.	Cö.?
	B'day?	194a?	Höchsterwünschtes Freudenfest	?	11 1 0		Some Cö. (?) pts.		Urform of BWV 194. Cf. 11/2/1723 and 6/4/1724	
		145/3+5							Urform of duet & aria of Cö. orig.?	Cö.?
		193a?	Ihr Häuser des Himmels . . .						Urform of Cö. orig.? Cf. 8/3/1727 (BWV 193)	
		120/4 (=120a/3)							Urform: a Cö. Sop aria? first parod. in BWV 1019a/3	

1723

Date	Occasion	BWV	Title	Text source	Nos.	Sources		Notes	Year
2/7	Estomihi = Quinqua-gesima	22	*Jesus nahm zu sich die Zwölfe*	?; 1: NT; 5: Kreuziger 1524	5 / 1 / 1*	E.Bn.+ copy by K₁	Unique + IMK	Probestück for Leipzig Cantorate	1723
		23	*Du wahrer Gott und Davids Sohn*	?; 4: German Agnus Dei 1528	4 or 2 1+ / 0 1*	W.Bn. E.Bn. JSB + K₁ + M	Cö. Wm. + IMK	4th mvt. added later in 1723	1723
5/16	Whits.	59?	*Wer mich liebet, der wird mein Wort halten I*	Neumeister; 1: NT; 3: Luther 1524	4(+1)[10] / 0 / 1(+1)	W.Bn. M / W.Bn.	Unique + IMK	Solo cant: S, B. Final chor. not ext. 1,4,3: parod. in BWV 74/1+2, 175/7, resp.	1716 or 1723

JAHRGANG[11] I

Date	Occasion	BWV	Title	Text source	Nos.	Sources		Notes	Year
5/30	1 p. Trin.	75	*Die Elenden sollen essen*	Weiss?; 1: Ps.22; 7+14: Rodigast 1674	14:7+7 / 1 / 2* id.	W.Bn.	Unique	Mvts. 7 + 14 = BWV 100/6	1723
6/6	2 p. Trin.	76	*Die Himmel erzählen die Ehre Gottes*	Weiss?; 1: Ps.19; 7+14: Luther 1524	14:7+7 / 1 / 2* id.	E.Bn. W.Bn. K₁ + M	IMK	Aut. date. 8: cf. BWV 528: Organ Sonata 4/1	1723
6/13	3 p. Trin.	(21)	*Ich hatte viel Bekümmernis*		11:6+5 / 4 / 0	E.Bn. 3rd set of pts:K₁+M	IMK	Rev. of Wei. cant. Cf. 1713, 1714, and 1720	1714
6/20	4 p. Trin.	(185)	*Barmherziges Herze der ewigen Liebe*		6 / 0 / 1(*)	W.Bn. E.Bn. K₁	IMK 2nd set of pts.	Rev. of Wei. cant. Cf. 7/14/1715	1715

10. The two parentheses (lines 1 and 3) have the following meaning: in the manuscript of the vocal bass part, the note "Chorale segue" appears after the 4th movement. Although the movement is missing, Neumeister's text permits an informed guess as to what chorale verse and melody may originally have been sung here (Cantata 6/6).

11. See above, p. 7, fn.2.

I Date	II Occasion	III BWV	IV Title	V Text	VI Mvts.	VII Score	VIII Pts. & Cop.	IX Wm.	X Remarks	XI Old Date
1723 (cont.)										
6/20		24	Ein ungefärbt Gemüte	Neumeister; 3: NT; 6: Heermann 1630	6 or / 1 2 / 1*0	W.Bn.	W.Bn. K_1+M	Both IMK		1723
6/24	St. John	167	Ihr Menschen, rühmet Gottes Liebe	?; 5: Gramann 1548	5 or / 1 0 / 0 1*		W.Bn. K_1	IMK	(Solo cant.): S,A,T,B	1723-27
6/27	5 p. Trin.	?	?							
Before 7/2	?	237	Sanctus in C			E.Bn.	W.Bn. K_1	IMK	authentic?	1723
7/2	Visitation	(147)	Herz und Mund und Tat und Leben	Franck 1717; 6+10: Jahn 1661: 2, 4, 8, 9: JSB?	10 / 1 / 2* id.	W.Bn.	W.Bn. K_2+M	IMK	147a enlarged by 3 rec. + new aria & chor. Cf. 12/20/1716	ca. 1727
7/4	6 p. Trin.	?								
7/11	7 p. Trin.	(186)	Ärgre dich, o Seele, nicht	Franck 1717; 6: Speratus 1524; 2, 4, 7, 9: JSB?	11 / 3:2 id. / 0	W.Bn. (Anon. Ih)		IMK	Dated 1723. 186a enlarged by 4 rec. + new chor.; Cf. 12/13 1716	1723
7/18	8 p. Trin.	136	Erforsche mich, Gott, und erfahre mein Herz	?; 1: Ps. 139; 6: Heermann 1630	6 / 1 (*)	[W.Bn.]	W.Bn. K_2+M	IMK	1: parod. in BWV 234	1723-27 or 1737/8?
7/18	Fun. Serv. (Vesper)	227	Jesu, meine Freude	Joh. Franck 1653 + NT	11 / 7 / 4:2 id.				Four 18th c. copies ext.	1723
7/25	9 p. Trin.	105	Herr, gehe nicht ins Gericht mit deinem Knecht	?; 1: Ps. 143; 6: Rist 1641	6 / 1 / 1*	E.Bn.		IMK		1723-27

10 p. Trin.	8/1	46	*Schauet doch und sehet, ob irgend ein Schmerz sei*	?; 1: OT; 6: Schnurr 1632	6 / 1 / 1*		W.Bn. K₂	IMK	1: parod. in BWV 232 (Qui tollis)	1723-27
11 p. Trin.	8/8	179	*Siehe zu, dass deine Gottesfurcht nicht Heuchelei sei*	Weiss?; 1: OT; 6: Tietze 1663	6 / 1 / 1	W.Bn.	[W.Bn.] K₂	IMK	1, 3; 5: parod. in BWV 236 & 234	1724
		(199)					[W.Bn.] M		Rev. of Wei. cant. Cf. 8/12/1714	
B'day: Duke Frederick II of Saxe-Gotha (at Lp. Univ.)	8/9	App. 20	Latin Ode. Text and music are lost.							
12 p. Trin.	8/15	69a	*Lobe den Herrn, meine Seele*	?; 1: Ps. 103; 6: Rodigast 1676	6 / 1 / 1		E.Bn. K₂+M	IMK	Urform of BWV 69	1724
13 p. Trin.	8/22	77	*Du sollst Gott, deinen Herren, lieben*	?; 1: NT; 6: Gesenius/Denicke 1657	6 / 1 / 1	W.Bn.		IMK		1723-27
14 p. Trin.	8/29	25	*Es ist nichts Gesundes an meinem Leibe*	?; 1: Ps. 38; 6: Heermann 1630	6 / 1 / 1		W.Bn. K₂+M	ma		ca. 1731
Inaug. of new Town Council	8/30	119	*Preise, Jerusalem, den Herrn*	?; 1: Ps. 147; 9: Luther 1529	9 / 2 / 1	W.Bn.		ma	Aut. date	1723
15 p. Trin.	9/5	138	*Warum betrübst du dich, mein Herz?*	?; 1, 3, 7: ? Nürnberg 1561	7 or / 3 0 / 0 3*	W.Bn.		ma? + IMK	5: parod. in BWV 236	Bef. 1737/8 (1732?)
16 p. Trin.	9/12	95	*Christus, der ist mein Leben*	?; 1: ? + Luther; 3: Herberger; 7: N. Herman 1560	7 / 1 / 1*		W. Bn. K₂+M	ma		1732

I Date	II Occasion	III BWV	IV Title	V Text	VI Mvts.	VII Score	VIII Pts. & Cop.	IX Wm.	X Remarks	XI Old Date
1723 (*cont.*)										
9/19	17 p. Trin.	?							See 9/23/1725	
9/26	18 p. Trin.	?								
9/29	St. Michael	50?	Nun ist das Heil und die Kraft	NT	1 1 0				Two 18th c. copies of sc. ext.	ca. 1740
10/3	19 p. Trin.	48	Ich elender Mensch, wer wird mich erlösen	?; 1: NT; 3: Rutilius 1604; 7:? 1620	7 1 2	E.Bn.	E.Bn. K_2+M	ma		ca. 1732
10/10	20 P. Trin.	(162)					W.Bn. K_2+M		Rev. of Wei. cant. Cf. 11/3/1715	
10/17	21 p. Trin.	109	Ich glaube, lieber Herr, hilf meinem Unglauben!	?; 1: NT; 6: Spengler 1524	6 or 2 1 0 1*	E.Bn.	E.Bn. K_2+M	ma		1727-36
10/24	22 p. Trin.	89	Was soll ich aus dir machen, Ephraim?	?; 1: OT; 6: Heermann 1630	6 0 1		W.Bn. K_2+M	ma	(Solo cant.): S,A,B	ca. 1732
10/31	23 p. Trin. & Reformation	(163?)							Reperform. of BWV 163?	
11/2	Organ Dedication (at Störmthal)	(194)	Höchster-wünschtes Freudenfest	?; 6: Heermann 1630, 12: Gerhardt 1647	12:6+6 1 2(*)	E.Bn.	W.Bn. K_2	ma + IMK	Rev. of Cö. sec. cant. Cf. 1717-23	1723
11/7	24 p. Trin.	60	O Ewigkeit, du Donnerwort II (Dialogus)	?; 1: Rist 1642; 4: NT; 5: Burmeister 1662	5 0 1		W.Bn. K_2	ma	(Solo cant.): A,T,B	1732
11/14	25. p. Trin.	90	Es reisset euch ein schrecklich Ende	?; 5: Moller 1584	5 0 1	E.Bn.		ma	(Solo cant.): A,T,B	ca. 1740

Date	Occasion	BWV	Title	Text sources	Nos.	E.Bn./W.Bn.	K	IMK	Notes	Year
11/21	26. p. Trin.	(70)	*Wachet! betet! betet! wachet!*	S. Franck 1717; 7: ? 1620; 11.: Keymann 1658; 2, 4, 6, 9: ?	11 11 1 1+1*		W.Bn. K₂+M	11 pts: IMK	70a enlarged by 4 rec. + 1 new chor. Cf. 12/20/1716	1723
11/28	1. Advent	(61)							Reperf. of Wei. cant. (?) Cf. 12/2/1714	
			[No cantatas from 2. Advent to Christmas]							
12/25	Xmas Day	(63)						2 pts: IMK	Reperf. of Wei. cant. Cf. 12/10/1713	
		243a	Magnificat (E-flat major version)	Luke 1:46-55; the 2 doxologies; Luther & Eber	16 7 1*	E.Bn.		IMK	"Virga Jesse" parod. in BWV 110/5	1723
		238?	Sanctus in D		2?	E.Bn.	W.Bn. K₂+M	IMK	or 1724?	ca. 1725
12/26	2. Xmas Day	40	*Dazu ist erschienen der Sohn Gottes*	JSB?; 1: NT; 3: Füger 1592; 6: Gerhardt 1653; 8: Keymann 1646	8 1 3	E.Bn.	W.Bn. K₂+M	IMK	1: parod. in BWV 233	1723
12/27	3. Xmas Day	64	*Sehet, welch eine Liebe hat uns der Vater erzeiget*	JSB?; 1: NT; 2: Luther 1524; 4: Pfefferkorn 1667; 8: J.Franck 1650	8 1 3		W.Bn. K₂+M	IMK	2,4: cf. BWV 91/6 and 94/8	1723
1724										
1/1	New Year	190	*Singet dem Herrn ein neues Lied!*	?; (Pic.?); 1: Ps; 7: J. Herman 1593	7 1 2*	[W.Bn.]	[W.Bn.] K₃	IMK	Urform of BWV 190a; only 2 Vn. pts. ext.	1724
1/2	Sun. p. New Year	153	*Schau, lieber Gott, wie meine Feind*	?; 1: Denicke 1646; 3: OT; 5: Gerhardt 1653; 9: Moller 1587	9 0 3		W.Bn. K₂+M	IMK	(Solo cant.): A,T,B	1724 or 1727

I Date	II Occasion	III BWV	IV Title	V Text	VI Mvts.	VII Score	VIII Pts. & Cop.	IX Wm.	X Remarks	XI Old Date
1724 (cont.)										
1/6	Epiph.	65	*Sie werden aus Saba alle kommen*	JSB? 1: OT; 2: German *Puer Natus* 1545; 7: Gerhardt 1647	7 1 2	E.Bn.		IMK		1724 or 1725
1/9	1 p. Epiph.	154	*Mein liebster Jesus ist verloren*	Weiss?; 3: Jahn 1661; 5: NT; 8: Keymann 1658	8 0 2	[E.Bn.] not aut.	E.Bn. sc: Ih; pts: K₂+M	IMK	(Solo cant.): A, T, B Orig. date. Rev. of Wei. cant.?	1724
1/16	2 p. Epiph.	(155)							Reperf. of Wei. cant? Cf. 1/19/1716	
1/23	3 p. Epiph.	73	*Herr, wie du willt, so schicks mit mir*	JSB?; 1: Bienemann 1582; 5: Helmbold 1563	5 1 1		W.Bn. K₃	IMK		1723-27
1/30	4 p. Epiph.	81	*Jesus schläft, was soll ich hoffen?*	Weiss?; 4: NT; 7: J. Franck 1650	7 0 1	E.Bn.	E.Bn. K₂+M	IMK	(Solo cant.): A, T, B	1724
2/2	Purification	83	*Erfreute Zeit im neuen Bunde*	?; 2: NT; 5: Luther 1524	5 0 1		W.Bn. K₂+M	IMK	(Solo cant.): A, T, B	1724
2/6	Septuagesima	144	*Nimm, was dein ist, und gehe hin*	?; 1: NT; 3: Rodigast 1674; 6: AvB 1547	6 1 2	E.Bn.		IMK		1723-27
2/13	Sexagesima	181	*Leichtgesinnte Flattergeister*	?	5 1 0		W.Bn. K₂+M	IMK	partly rev.?	1723-27
		(18)?					E.Bn. M	3 pts: IMK	Reperf. in A minor Cf. 2/19/1713	

Date	Occasion	Title	Text	Nos.	Instr.	Parts	Remarks	Year
2/20	Estomihi (23)?				E.Bn. K_2+M	Some: IMK	Reperf. (?) in B minor & with 4th mvt. Cf. 2/7/1723	

[No church cantatas from Estomihi to Palm Sunday i.e. during Lent]

Date	Occasion	Title	Text	Nos.	Instr.	Parts	Remarks	Year
3/25	Annunciation (182)				E.Bn. 10 pts: K_2	IMK	Reperf. of Wei. cant. Cf. 3/25/1714	
4/7	Good Friday 245	St. John Passion	Brockes & Bach; NT: John + 11 hymns	68 / 16: 2 id. / 11	E.Bn. M, etc.	Oldest pts: IMK	1st version	1723
4/9	Easter (31?)						Reperf. of Wei. cant. Cf. 4/21/1715	
4/9	Easter (4)	Christ lag in Todesbanden	Luther 1524	8 / 1 (+1)?[12] / 1	Lp. M + C	9 pts: IMK	Reperf. & rev. of Mühlh. cantata. Cf. 4/24/1707	1724 (or Wei.?)
4/10	2. Easter Day (66)?	Erfreut euch, ihr Herzen (Dialogus)	? (JSB?); 6: Easter hymn ca. 1200	6 / 1 / 1	E.Bn.	ZVM Wm. of 1734/5	Parod. of 66a: Cö. Cf. 12/10/1718. Text print. Lp., 1731	1731
4/11	3. Easter Day (134)	Ein Herz, das seinen Jesum lebend weiss	? (JSB?)	6 / 1 / 0	W.Bn. E.Bn. M + K_2	partly IMK	Parod. of 134a: Cö. Cf. 1/1/1719. Text print. Lp., 1731	1731
4/16	Quasimodo-geniti 67	Halt im Gedächtnis Jesum Christ	Weiss?; 1, 2: NT: 4: Herman 1560; 7: Ebert 1601	7 / 1 / 2	E.Bn. K_2 + M	IMK	6: parod. in BWV 234	1723-27

12. As **colla parte** instruments double the voices in the opening chorale fantasy and the closing simple chorale harmonization (*versus* 1 and 7), there can be no question as to choral performance of these movements. On the other hand, the absence of *colla parte* instruments in *versus* 4 points to solo execution of this movement in Bach's time.

I Date	II Occasion	III BWV	IV Title	V Text	VI Mvts.	VII Score	VIII Pts. & Cop.	IX Wm.	X Remarks	XI Old Date
1724 (cont.)										
4/23	Misericordia Domini	104	*Du Hirte Israel, höre*	Weiss?; 1: Ps. 80; 6: Becker 1598	6 / 1 / 1		W.Bn. K₃ + M	IMK		1723-27
4/27		App. 15	*Siehe, der Hüter Israel*						Listed in Breitkopf catalogue 1761	
4/30	Jubilate	(12)					W.Bn. M	2 pts: IMK	Reperf. of Wei. cant. Cf. 4/22/1714	
5/7	Cantate	166	*Wo gehest du hin?*	Weiss?; 1: NT; 3: Ringwaldt 1582; 6: ÄJvS-R 1688	6 / 0 / 1		W.Bn. K₃ + M etc.	IMK	(Solo cant.): A, T, B. 2: cf. Organ Trio, BWV 584	1723-27
5/14	Rogate	86	*Wahrlich, wahrlich, ich sage euch*	Weiss?; 1: NT; 3: Grünwald 1530; 6: Speratus 1524	6 / 0 / 1	E.Bn.		IMK	(Solo cant.): S, A, T, B	1723-27
5/18	Ascension	37	*Wer da gläubet und getauft wird*	Weiss?; 1: NT; 3: Nicolai 1599; 6: Kolrose 1535	6 / 1 / 1		W. Bn. 3 diff. + K: t.p.	3 pts: IMK	Cf. 1731: cop. Krebs; Wm.: MA	ca. 1729
5/21	Exaudi	44	*Sie werden euch in den Bann tun I*	Weiss?; 1, 2: NT; 4: Moller 1587; 7: Fleming 1642	7 / 1 / 1	E.Bn.	W.Bn. K₃ + M etc.	IMK		1723-27
5/28	1. Whits.	(172) (59)							Cf. 5/20/1714 Cf. 5/16/1723	

Before Bach launches his most sustained creative effort, the Chorale Cantatas of Jahrgang II, he fills the three Whitsuntide Days and Trinity with re-performances, revisions and parodies of Weimar and Cöthen cantatas, even an earlier Leipzig one. They are documented by parts bearing the characteristic IMK watermark and by Bach's copyists of this time: K₃ and/or M (in the case of BWV 165 by a copy of the score: watermark IMK, copyist J. C. Köpping).

22

							See below: About 1728			
5/29	2. Whits.	(173)?	Erhöhtes Fleisch und Blut	JSB?	6 1 0				Parod. of 173a; Cf. 12/10/1722?	ca. 1730
5/30	3. Whits.	(184)	Erwünschtes Freudenlicht	JSB?; 5: A. von Wildenfels 1527?	6 1 1	W.Bn. not aut. t.p.: JSB	W.Bn. JSB, K₃+M	IMK + Unicorn	Parod. of 184a;cf. 1/1/1723. 6A = BWV 213/13A	1724 or 1731
6/4	Trin.	(194)							See: 1717-23 + 11/2/1723	
	ca. Whits.?	(165)							See: 6/16/1715	
		App.24	Mass in A minor			E.Bn.	W.Bn. M	IMK	Of doubtful authenticity	

JAHRGANG II

							About 1728			
6/11	1 p. Trin.	20	O Ewigkeit, du Donnerwort I	1,7,11: Rist 1642;the other verses par. by JSB?	11:7+4 1 2 id.	Pr. N.Y.	Lp. K₃	2 pts: IMK; rest: Halfmoon[13]		1723-27
6/18	2 p. Trin.	2	Ach Gott, vom Himmel sieh darein	1,6:Luther 1524; 2-5 par: by JSB?	6 1 1	Pr. N.Y.	Lp. K₃+M	)		1735-44
6/24	St. John	7	Christ unser Herr zum Jordan kam	1,7:Luther 1541; 2-6: par. by JSB?	7 1 1		Lp. K₃			1735-44
6/25	3 p. Trin.	135	Ach Herr, mich armen Sünder	1,6:Schneegass 1597; 2-5:par. by JSB?	6 1 1	Lp.	IMK +)			1735-44
7/2	4 p. Trin. & Visitation	10	Meine Seel erhebt den Herren	1,5,7: German Magnificat; 2-4, 6:par.by JSB?	7 1 1	LC	Lp. K₃+M	)	5: cf. BWV 648, Schübler Organ Chorale No. 4	1735-44

13. The famous watermark of the 2nd Jahrgang, which Spitta misinterpreted so fatefully (see column: *Old Date!*); from here on shown as:) .

I Date	II Occasion	III BWV	IV Title	V Text	VI Mvts.	VII Score	VIII Pts. & Cop.	IX Wm.	X Remarks	XI Old Date
1724 (cont.)										
7/9	5 p. Trin.	93	Wer nur den lieben Gott lässt walten	1,4,5,7:Neumark 1657; 2,3,6: par. by JSB?	7 / 1		Lp. IIa	) only 1 folio	See 1732/35. 4: cf. BWV 647: Schübler Chor. 3	1728
7/16	6 p. Trin.	?								
7/23	7 p. Trin.	107	Was willst du dich betrüben	Heermann 1630	7 / 1 / 1		Lp. K₃ + M	Mostly)		ca.1735
7/30	8 p. Trin.	178	Wo Gott, der Herr, nicht bei uns hält	Jonas 1524 (after Ps.124); 3,6: par. by JSB?	7 / 1 / 1+1*		Lp. + Pr. K₃	Mostly)		1735-44
8/6	9 p. Trin.	94	Was frag ich nach der Welt	Pfefferkorn 1667; 2,4,6: par. by JSB? 7: JSB?	8 / 1 / 1	E.Bn.	Lp. K₃	sc:) pts: Eagle + H	8: cf. BWV 64/4; Cf. 12/27/1723	1735
8/13	10 p. Trin.	101	Nimm von uns, Herr, du treuer Gott	Moller 1584; 2,4,6: par. by JSB?	7 / 1 / 1		Lp. K₃	Eagle + H		1735-44
8/20	11 p. Trin.	113	Herr Jesu Christ, du höchstes Gut	Ringwaldt 1588; 3-7: par by JSB?	8 / 1 / 1	Pr. N.Y.		Eagle + H		1735-44
8/27	12 p. Trin.	?								
8/28	Inaug. of new Town Council	?								
9/3	13 p. Trin.	33	Allein zu dir, Herr Jesu Christ	1,6: Hubert 1540; 2-5: par. by JSB?	6 / 1 / 1	Pr. USA	Lp. K₃ + M, etc.	Eagle + H		1735-44
9/10	14 p. Trin.	78	Jesu, der du meine Seele	1,7: Rist 1641; 2-6: par. by JSB?	7 / 1 / 1		Lp. K₃, JSB, M etc.	Eagle + H		1735-44

Date	Occasion	No.	Title	Chorale text	Mvts.	Source	Copyist	Remarks	Date
9/17	15 p. Trin.	99	Was Gott tut, das ist wohlgetan II	1,6: Rodigast 1674; 2-5: par. by JSB?	6 1 1	NA	Eagle + H	1: (+ horn & k. drums) = BWV 100/1	ca. 1733
9/24	16 p. Trin.	8	Liebster Gott, wann werd ich sterben?	1,6: Neumann bef.1697; 2-5: par. by JSB?	6 1 1(?)	Lp. & Bruss. M	)	E major version (version in D: late Lp. period)	ca. 1724
9/29	St. Michael	130	Herr Gott, dich loben alle wir	1,6: Eber ca.1561; 2-5: par. by JSB?	6 1 1(*)	Pr. W. Germ.	disp. M + WF[14])		1735-44
10/1	17 p. Trin.	114	Ach, lieben Christen, seid getrost	1,4,7: Gigas 1561; 2,3,5,6: par. by JSB?	7 1 1	Pr. NY	Lp. K₃)		1735-44 (or ca. 1745?)
10/8	18 p. Trin.	96	Herr Christ, der einge Gottessohn	1,6: Kreuziger 1524; 2-5: par. by JSB?	6 1 1	E.Bn.	Lp. K₃ + M)	Reperf.: 10/24/1734 and 1744-48	1735-44
10/15	19 p. Trin.	5	Wo soll ich fliehen hin	1,7: Heermann 1630; 2-6: par. by JSB?	7 1 1	Pr. Ln.	Lp. K₃ + M)	Reperf.: 1732-35	1735 (or 1745?)
10/22	20 p. Trin.	180	Schmücke dich, o liebe Seele	1,3,7: J.Franck 1653; 2,4-6: par. by JSB?	7 1 1	Pr. USA	)		1735-44
10/29	21 p. Trin.	38	Aus tiefer Not schrei ich zu dir	1,4,6: Luther 1524; 2,3,5: par. by JSB?	6 1 1		Lp. K₃ + M)		1735-44
10/31	Reformation	(80)?	Ein feste Burg ist unser Gott	1,2,5,8: Luther 1529; 3,4,6,7: S.Franck 1715	8 1(+1) 1	three 18th c. copies		80a rev. and enlarg. by mvts. 1+5; cf. 3/24/1715	1730 (or 1739?)
		(76)?				W.Bn.	1 pt:)	Reperf. of Pt.II?	
11/5	22 p. Trin.	115	Mache dich, mein Geist, bereit	1,6: Freystein 1697; 2-5: par. by JSB?	6 1 1	Cambr. t.p.: K	)		1735-44

14. Wilhelm Friedmann, not quite 14 years of age, appears here for the first time as copyist of his father's cantata manuscripts.

I Date	II Occasion	III BWV	IV Title	V Text	VI Mvts.	VII Score	VIII Pts. & Cop.	IX Wm.	X Remarks	XI Old Date
1724 (cont.)										
11/12	23 p. Trin.	139	Wohl dem, der sich auf seinen Gott	1,6: Rüben 1692; 2-5: par. by JSB?	6 1 1		Lp. K_3 + M	9 pts:)		1735-44
11/19	24 p. Trin.	26	Ach wie flüchtig, ach wie nichtig	1,6: M.Franck 1652; 2-5: par. by JSB?	6 1 1	E.Bn.	Lp. K_3 + AM^{15} + JSB	)		1735-44
11/26	25 p. Trin.	116	Du Friedefürst, Herr Jesu Christ	1,6: Ebert 1601; 2-5:par. by JSB?	6 1 1	Paris t.p.: K	[Lp.] K_3, M, JSB	)	Cont. pt. in Château de Mariemont	1745
12/3	1. Advent	62	Nun komm, der Heiden Heiland II	1,6: Luther 1524: 2-5: par. by JSB?	6 1 1	W.Bn. t.p:K	Lp. K_4 + M, etc.	)	Reperf.: 1732-35	1735-44
				[No cantatas from 2. Advent to Christmas]						
12/25	Xmas Day	91	Gelobet seist du, Jesu Christ	1,2,6: Luther 1524; 3-5: par. by JSB?	6 1 1(*)	W.Bn.	Lp. K_4 + WF, etc.	mostly)	2 later reperf. documented. 6: cf.BWV 64/2	1735-44
		232/III	Sanctus in D (of the later B-minor Mass)		2 2 0	W.Bn.	Anon. IIf,IIg	sc:) 3 pts:)	Reperf. 1726 or 1727. Cf. also: ca. 1748	1733
12/26	2. Xmas Day	121	Christum wir sollen loben schon	1,6: Luther 1524: par. by JSB?	6 1 1	NA	Lp. K_4+M, C	)		1735-44
12/27	3. Xmas Day	133	Ich freue mich in dir	1,6: K.Ziegler 1697; 2-5: par. by JSB?	6 1 1	E.Bn.	Lp. K_3, M+ WF	mostly)		1735 or 1737
12/31	Sun. p. Xmas	122	Das neugeborne Kindelein	1,4,6:Schneegass 1597; 2-5: par. by JSB?	6 1 1	W.Bn.	Lp. K_4 + C	)		ca. 1742

1725

								Reperf. 1732-35. 6: = BWV 171/6	1735/36?
1/1	New Year	41	*Jesus, nun sei gepreiset*	1,6: J.Herman 1593; 2-5: par. by JSB?	6 1 1*	[W.Bn.]	Lp. K, + M, etc.	)	
1/6	Epiph.	123	*Liebster Immanuel, Herzog der Frommen*	1,6: Fritsch 1679; 2-5: par. by JSB?	6 1 1	NA	Lp. K, M, C + WF	)	1735-44
1/7	1. p. Epiph.	124	*Meinen Jesum lass ich nicht*	1,6: Keymann 1658; 2-5: par. by JSB?	6 1 1	W.Bn.	Lp. K, M, AM, WF,	)	1735-44
1/14	2 p. Epiph.	3	*Ach Gott, wie manches Herzeleid I*	1,2,6: Moller 1587; (2), 3-5: par. by JSB?	6 1 1+1?	Pr. Switz.	Lp. K, C, + WF	)	1735-44
1/21	3 p. Epiph.	111	*Was mein Gott will, das g'scheh allzeit*	1,6: AvB 1547; 2-5: par. by JSB?	6 1 1	NA	[W.Bn.] AM,WF, K: t.p.	)	1735-44 Only duplicate pts. are ext.
1/28	Septuagesima	92	*Ich hab in Gottes Herz und Sinn*	Gerhardt 1647; 3,5,6,8: par. by JSB?	9 1 1+1?	W.Bn.	Lp. K, C + WF	)	1735-44
2/2	Purification	125	*Mit Fried und Freud ich fahr dahin*	1,3,6: Luther 1524; 2-5: par. by JSB?	6 1 1		Lp. K, M, + WF	)	1735-44
2/4	Sexagesima	126	*Erhalt uns, Herr, bei deinem Wort*	1,3:Luther 1524; 6: Luther 1529; 2,4,5: par. by JSB?	6 1 1		Lp. K, M, C + WF	)	1735-44
2/11	Estomihi	127	*Herr Jesu Christ, wahr' Mensch und Gott*	1,5: Eber 1562; 2-4: par. by JSB?	5 1 1	W.Bn.	Lp. K, + WF	)	1735-44

15. First appearance of Anna Magdalena's handwriting in copies of cantatas by her husband.

I Date	II Occasion	III BWV	IV Title	V Text	VI Mvts.	VII Score	VIII Pts. & Cop.	IX Wm.	X Remarks	XI Old Date
1725 *(cont.)*										
2/12	Wedding: Lösner/ Scherling	App.14	*Sein Segen fliesst daher wie ein Strom*		6 0 0				Only text ext: Lp, 1725	1725
2/23	B'day: Duke of Saxe-Weissenfels	249a	*Entfliehet, ver-schwindet, ent-weichet, ihr Sorgen*	Pic.¹⁰ (printed 1727)	10 (1) 0	Music lost; text ext.			Urform of Easter Orat.BWV 249; Solo cant:S,A,T,B	1725
[No church cantatas from Estomihi to Palm Sunday]										
3/25	Palm Sunday (& Annunciation)	1	*Wie schön leuchtet der Morgenstern*	1,6: Nicolai 1599; 2-5: par. by JSB?	6 1(*)		Lp, K, M, C + WF	Sw.I	Last Chorale Cant. of Jahrgang II	1735-44 or 1733/4?
3/30	Good Friday	(245)	St. John Passion (2nd version)			E.Bn.	K,M,C	Some pts: Sw.I	Rev. of 1st version; cf. 4/7/1724	2nd perf. 1727
4/1	Easter	249	*Kommt, eilet und laufet* (Easter Oratorio)	Pic.?	10 1 0	W.Bn. (but of 1732-35)	W.Bn. K, M	1st set: Sw.I	Parody of 249a; cf. 2/23/1725	ca.1736
		(4)					Lp. M + C	4 pts: Sw.I	4 wind pts. added; cf. 4/9/1724 and 4/24/1707	
4/2	2. Easter Day	6	*Bleib bei uns, denn es will Abend werden*	Weiss?; 1: NT; 3:after Melanchthon; 6:Luther 1542	6 1 1	W.Bn.	E.Bn. K,M,C	sc:) pts: Sw.I	3: cf. BWV 649: Schübler Organ Chorale No. 5	1736?
4/3	3. Easter Day	(4)?							See above:4/1/1725	
4/8	Quasimodo-geniti	42	*Am Abend aber desselbigen Sabbats*	Weiss?; 2: NT; 4: Fabricius ca. 1635; 7:Luther 1524	7 0 1	E.Bn.	E.Bn. K4, C, + WF	Sw.I	(Solo cant): S,A,T,B 2 later reperf.	1731

28

Date	Occasion	BWV	Title	Text source					Notes	Year
4/15	Misericordia Domini	85	Ich bin ein guter Hirt	Weiss?, 1; NT; 3:Becker 1598; 6:Homburg 1658	6 0 1	E.Bn.	K, M,C, + WF		Mostly Sw.I; 2 pts:)	(Solo cant.): S,A,T,B	1735
4/22	Jubilate	103	Ihr werdet weinen und heulen	MvZ,[17] rev. by JSB?, 1: NT; 6:Gerhardt 1653	6 1 1	E.Bn.	W.Bn. K, WF	sc: Sw.I pts: RS	Reperf. 1731	1735
4/29	Cantate	108	Es ist euch gut, dass ich hingehe	MvZ, 1,4: NT; 6: Gerhardt 1653	6 1 1	E.Bn.	W.Bn. K, WF, + JSB	)+ RS		1735
April or May?	B'day of a teacher	36c	Schwingt freudig euch empor	Pic.?	9 2 0	E.Bn.		RS	Cf. BWV 36a: 11/30/1726;BWV 36: 12/2/1731; BWV 36b: 1735?	1733/34
5/6	Rogate	87	Bisher habt ihr nichts gebeten in meinem Namen	MvZ, rev. by JSB?; 1,5: NT; 7:H.Müller 1659	6 0 1	E.Bn.	E.Bn. K, JSB, M, WF	)+ RS	(Solo cant.): A,T,B	1735
5/10	Ascension	128	Auf Christi Himmelfahrt allein	MvZ, rev. by JSB?; 1:Wegelin-Sonnemann 1661; 5: Avenarius 1673	5 1 1 (*)	Pr. Switz.	W.Bn. K, WF, M etc.	RS		1735
5/13	Exaudi	183	Sie werden euch in den Bann tun II	MvZ, rev.by JSB?; 1: NT;5: Gerhardt 1653	5 0 1	E.Bn.	W.Bn. K, etc.	RS	(Solo cant): S,A,T,B	1735
5/20	1. Whits.	74	Wer mich liebet, der wird mein Wort halten II	MvZ; 1,4,6: NT; 8: Gerhardt 1653	8 1 1		W.Bn. K, C, M, WF	RS	1,2 = BWV 59/ 1+4 revised	1735 (or 1731?)
5/21	2. Whits.	68	Also hat Gott die Welt geliebt	MvZ; 1: Liscow 1675; 5: NT	5 2 0		Lp. K, M, JSB	RS	4, 2: = BWV 208/7+13 (also V/5) revised	1735

16. First documented appearance of Picander (Christian Friedrich Henrici) as poet of a text set to music by Bach.

17. First appearance of the Leipzig poetess Mariane von Ziegler.

I Date	II Occasion	III BWV	IV Title	V Text	VI Mvts.	VII Score	VIII Pts. & Cop.	IX Wm.	X Remarks	XI Old Date
1725 (cont.)										
5/22	3. Whits.	175	*Er rufet seinen Schafen mit Namen*	MvZ, rev.by JSB?; 1,5:NT; 7: Rist 1651	7 0 1(*)	E.Bn.	W.Bn. K, C, + WF	RS	(Solo cant): A,T,B 4,7 = BWV 173a/7 & 59/3 rev'd	1735 or 1736
5/27	Trin.	176	*Es ist ein trotzig und verzagt Ding*	MvZ,rev.by JSB?,1: OT,6: Gerhardt 1653	6 1 1	E.Bn.	Pr. USA K₄	RS		ca.1735 (or 1732?)

JAHRGANG III

On March 25, 1725, Bach ceased writing chorale cantatas, and two months later on May 27, 1725, he brought the steady flow of cantata composition to a halt. Bach was never to revive the regularity of composition for the service of his church that had characterized his first two years in Leipzig. This sudden cessation of creative activity still baffles Bach scholars.[18]

Inasmuch as Jahrgang I and II have shown the complete calendar of the Leipzig church year, hereafter only performances of new vocal works will be listed with full accompanying evidence. Re-performances and revisions of earlier compositions, as well as performances of vocal music by other composers, will appear in summary fashion and abbreviated form.

From 1 through 8 p. Trin. (6/3–7/22) : no performances traceable.[19]

I Date	II Occasion	III BWV	IV Title	V Text	VI Mvts.	VII Score	VIII Pts. & Cop.	IX Wm.	X Remarks	XI Old Date
7/29	9 p. Trin.	168?	*Tue Rechnung! Donnerwort*	S.Franck 1715; 6: Ringwaldt 1588	6 0 1	E.Bn.	[Pr.,NY, W.Bn., Cambr.] K₄ + M	S.CoA, GAW	Urform: Wei.? (Solo cant): S,A,T,B	1723 or 24
8/3	Name Day: Lp. Univ. Prof. Müller	205	*Der zufriedengestellte Äolus*	Pic.	15 2 0	E.Bn.		S.CoA	Cf. 2/19/1734 Parody: BWV 205a	1725
8/5 & 12 (10 and 11 p. Trin.) : ?[19]										
8/19	12 p. Trin.	137	*Lobe den Herren, den mächtigen König der Ehren*	J. Neander 1680	5 1 1(*)		Lp. K₄	RS	Reperf. 1744-47; 2: cf. BWV 650: Schübler Chor. #6; 5: cf. 120a/8	1732 (1732-47?)

8/26	13 p. Trin.	164	*Ihr, die ihr euch von Christo nennet*	S.Franck 1715; 6: Kreuziger 1524	6 0 1	W.Bn.	E.Bn. K, M, WF etc.	GAW	(Solo cant.): S,A,T,B. Hardly of Wei. orig. 6: = BWV 132/6 ?	1723 or 24
8/27 through 9/16 (Inaug. of new Town Council—16 p. Trin.):?										
9/23	17 p. Trin.	148?	*Bringet dem Herrn Ehre seines Namens*	Pic., rev. by JSB?; 1: Ps.96; 6:Heermann 1630	6 1 1	W.Bn. (not aut.)			Already 1723? Copy (sc.) by Altnikol	1725
9/29 through 10/28 (St. Michael's Day—22 p. Trin.):?										
10/31	Reformation	79	*Gott der Herr ist Sonn und Schild*	Weiss ?; 1: Ps.; 3:Rinkart 1636; 6:Helmbold 1575	6:3+3 1 2*	W.Bn. E.Bn.	K,C, WF	RS + IAI	Reperf.: 1728-31. 1.5; 2: cf. BWV 236; 234.	1735 (?)
11/4 through 11/25 (23-26 p. Trin.):?										
11/27	Wedding: Hohenthal/ Mencke	I	*Auf! süss ent- zückende Gewalt*	Gottsched	13 (1?) 0				Only text ext. 3, 5: parod. in BWV 11/4 & 10	
12/2	1. Advent:	?								
12/25	Xmas Day	110	*Unser Mund sei voll Lachens*	Lehms; 1,3: OT; 5: NT; 7: Füger 1592	7 1 1	E.Bn.	E.Bn. K, JSB, M etc.	Sw.II	1: Rev.of BWV 1069/1; 5: of 243a: *Virga Jesse.*	bef.1734
12/26	2. Xmas Day	57	*Selig ist der Mann* (Dialogus)	Lehms; 1: OT; 8: Fritsch 1668	8 0 1	E.Bn.	W.Bn. K, M, + WF	Sw.II	(Solo cant): S,B	ca.1740
12/27	3. Xmas Day	151	*Süsser Trost, mein Jesus kömmt*	Lehms; 5: N. Herman 1560	5 0 1	Cob.	E.Bn. + Cob. K,C,WF,AM	Sw.II	Reperf.:1728-31. (Solo cant):S,A,T,B	1735-40

18. For an attempted yet inconclusive explanation see G. Herz, *op. cit.*, pp. 12/13.

19. It may be assumed that Bach repeated his cantatas of Jahrgang II.

I Date	II Occasion	III BWV	IV Title	V Text	VI Mvts.	VII Score	VIII Pts. & Cop.	IX Wm.	X Remarks	XI Old Date
1725 (cont.)										
12/30	Sun. p. Xmas	28	Gottlob! nun geht das Jahr zu Ende	Neumeister; 2: Gramann 1530; 3: OT; 6: Eber ca. 1580	6 / 1 / 1	E.Bn.	W.Bn. K, M, C, WF	Sw.II	2: a cap. version: BWV 231	1723-27 (ca.1736?)
1726										
1/1	New Year	16	Herr Gott, dich loben wir	Lehms; 1: Luther 1529; 6: Eber ca. 1580	6 / 2 / 1	E.Bn.	E.Bn. C, M etc.	Sw.II	Reperf.: 1728-31 and ca. 1748(?)	1724 (Wei.?)
1/6	Epiph.	?								
1/13	1. p. Epiph.	32	Liebster Jesu, mein Verlangen (Dialogus)	Lehms; 6: Gerhardt 1647	6 / 0 / 1	E.Bn.	E.Bn. C, AM, WF	Sw.II	(Solo cant): S,B Cö. Urform?	ca.1740 (1738?)
1/20	2 p. Epiph.	13	Meine Seufzer, meine Tränen	Lehms; 3: Heermann 1636; 6: Fleming 1642	6 / 0 / 1	E.Bn.	E.Bn. C, AM, WF	Sw.II	(Solo cant): S,A,T,B	ca.1740
1/27	3 p. Epiph.	72	Alles nur nach Gottes Willen	S.Franck 1715; 6:AvB 1547	6 / 1 / 1	E.Bn.	[E.Bn.] C, AM, WF	Sw.II	Urform of Wei. orig.?	1723-25 (or Cö. or Wei.?)

2/2 through 3/3 (Purification—Estomihi): Cantatas 9 and 1–5[20] by JSB's Meiningen cousin Johann Ludwig Bach were copied and performed by JSB!

I Date	II Occasion	III BWV	IV Title	V Text	VI Mvts.	VII Score	VIII Pts. & Cop.	IX Wm.	X Remarks	XI Old Date
2/4	Mem. Serv. (Motet) for Mrs. Winkler?	228?	Fürchte dich nicht	OT; Gerhardt 1653	1				Survives in 5 18th c. copies	1723-34
3/6	Wedding	34a	O ewiges Feuer, o Ursprung der Liebe	Weiss?	7 / 3 / 0		[E.Bn.] C, M, WF	Sw.II	Urform of BWV 34. Sources: incomplete	after 1734 (or ca. 1730)

[No church cantatas during Lent]

Date	Occasion	No.	Title	Text	Mvts	Sources	Score	Notes	Year
3/25	Annunciation ?								
4/19	Good Friday		Reinhard Keiser's Mark Passion				IAI	Already perf'd in Wei.:3/30/1714	
4/21 through 5/19 (Easter—Cantate Sunday): BWV 15[21] and Johann Ludwig Bach's cantatas 10, 11, 6, 12, 8? and 14.									
5/12	Jubilate	146?	Wir müssen durch viel Trübsal in das Reich Gottes eingehen	Pic.?; 2: NT; 8: ?	8 / 1 / 1	E.Bn. C, M	IAI	Or 1727-31? (2 18th c. copies ext.) 1,2 = BWV 1052/ 1+2 rev'd.	ca.1740
5/26	Rogate	?							
5/30	Ascension	43	Gott fähret auf mit Jauchzen	?; 1: Ps.47; 4: NT; 11: Rist 1641	11:5+6 / 1 / 1	E.Bn. C, M, JSB etc. W.Bn.	IAI + Sw.II		1735
6/2 through 6/11 (Exaudi—3. Whits.):?									
6/16	Trin.	(194)?				[W.Bn.]	Cont.: Sw.II	Reperf. of mvts. 12, 2-5, 7 & 10. Cf. 11/2/1723	
		or 129?	Gelobet sei der Herr, mein Gott	J.Olearius 1665	5 (or 2 1+ 0 1*)	Lp. C, M	ICF	Or: 10/31/1726, resp. 6/8 (= Trin.) 1727?	1732

JAHRGANG IV

Date	Occasion	No.	Title	Text	Mvts	Sources	Score	Notes	Year
6/23	1 p. Trin.	39	Brich dem Hungrigen dein Brot	?; 1,4: OT; 7: Denicke 1648	7:3+4 / 1 / 1	E.Bn. C, M	ICF + Sw.II, GM		1732?
6/24 and 7/2 (St. John's Day and Visitation): Joh. Ludwig Bach's cantatas 17 and 13.									
6/30, 7/7 and 7/14 (2, 3, and 4 p. Trin.):?									
7/21	5 p. Trin.	88	Siehe, ich will viel Fischer aussenden	?; 1: OT; 4: NT; 7: Neumark 1657	7:3+4 / 0 / 1	W.Bn. M, C	ICF	(Solo cant): S,A,T,B	1732

20. See BG 41, pp. 275-76, and Dürr in *Bach-Jahrbuch* 1957, 85-90.   21. Not by JSB but also by Johann Ludwig Bach.

I Date	II Occasion	III BWV	IV Title	V Text	VI Mvts.	VII Score	VIII Pts. & Cop.	IX Wm.	X Remarks	XI Old Date
1726 (cont.)										
7/28	6 p. Trin.	170	*Vergnügte Ruh, beliebte Seelenlust*	Lehms	5 0 0	W.Bn.	W.Bn. M	ICF	Solo cant.: A. Reperf. in 1740s	1731 or 1732
			Also: Joh. Ludwig Bach's cantata 7							
8/4	7 p. Trin.	187	*Es wartet alles auf dich*	?; 1: Ps. 104; 4: NT; 7: Erfurt 1563	7:3+4 1 1	E.Bn.	[W.Bn.+ Pr. USA] C, M	ICF	1,3,4,5: cf. BWV 235	1732
8/11	8 p. Trin.	45	*Es ist dir gesagt, Mensch, was gut ist*	?; 1: OT; 4: NT; 7: Heermann 1630	7:3+4 1 1	E.Bn.	W.Bn. C, M	ICF		1735-44
8/18	9 p. Trin.	?								
8/25	10 p. Trin.	102	*Herr, deine Augen sehen nach dem Glauben*	?; 1: OT; 4: NT; 7: Heermann 1630	7:4+3 1 1	E.Bn.	[E.Bn.] M, C	? (unique?)	Reperf.:ca.1737; 1;3;5: cf. BWV 235; & 233	1731 (or 32?)
8/25	B'day: Count von Flemming	(249b)	*Veriaget, zerstreuet, zerrüttet, ihr Sterne*	Pic. (printed 1727)	10 (1) 0				Parody of 249a Cf. 2/23/1725 Solo cant.:S,A,T,B	1726
8/26	Inaug. of new Town Council	(193)	*Ihr Tore zu Zion*	?	7 2 id. 0		W.Bn. C, WF	Sw.II+ S.CoA	Incomplete Cf. 193a:Cö. & 8/3/1727	1738?
9/1	11 p. Trin.		Joh. Ludwig Bach's cantata 15				W.Bn. M, C	GAW		
9/8	12 p. Trin.	35	*Geist und Seele wird verwirret*	Lehms	7:4+3 0 0	W.Bn.	E.Bn. C, M, WF?	sc:GAW pts: ICF	Solo cant: A (+ organ) 1,2,5: cf. BWV 1059/1 (+ 1059/2 & 3?)	1731
9/15	13 p. Trin.		Joh. Ludwig Bach's cantata 16				C, M	ICF		

Date	Occasion	BWV	Title	Text sources			Parts		Score	Notes	Date
9/22	14 p. Trin.	17	*Wer Dank opfert, der preiset mich*	?; 1: Ps 50; 4: NT; 7: Gramann 1530	7:3+4; 1; 1		E.Bn.	W.Bn. M, C	GAW, GM, S.CoA	1: cf. BWV 236	bef.1737 (1732?)
9/29	15 p. Trin. (= St. Michael)	19	*Es erhub sich ein Streit*	Pic., rev. by JSB?; 7: ? ca. 1620	7; 1; 1(*)		E.Bn.	W.Bn. C, M etc.	GM, ICF		1725 or 1726
10/6	16 p. Trin.	27	*Wer weiss, wie nahe mir mein Ende!*	?; 1: ÄJvS-R 1695; 3: Neumeister; 6:Albinus 1649	6; 1; 1?		W.Bn.	W.Bn. C	GM, ICF	Reperf.: 1737(?)	1731
10/13	17 p. Trin.	47	*Wer sich selbst erhöhet, der soll erniedriget werden*	Helbig 1720; 1: NT; 5: ? ca. 1560	5; 1; 1		E.Bn.	E.Bn. C, M	ICF	Reperf. 1734 or later	1720
10/20	18 p. Trin.	169	*Gott soll allein mein Herze haben*	?; 7: Luther 1524	7; 0; 1		W.Bn.	W.Bn. C	SW, ICF	(Solo cant):A (+ organ); 1,5: cf. BWV 1053/1 & 2	1731 (or 1732?)
10/27	19 p. Trin.	56	*Ich will den Kreuzstab gerne tragen*	rev. of Neumeister?; 5: J.Franck 1653	5; 0; 1		W.Bn.	W.Bn. M, C	S.CoA, ICF	(Solo cant): B	1731 or 1732
10/31	Reformation		?							BWV 129? Cf. 6/16/1726	
11/3	20 p. Trin.	49	*Ich geh und suche mit Verlangen (Dialogus)*	Pic.?; 6: Nicolai 1599	6; 0; 0		E.Bn.	E.Bn. C. M	ICF,) + S.CoA	Solo cant.:S, B (+ org.) 1: cf. BWV 1053/3	1731
11/10	21 p. Trin.	98	*Was Gott tut, das ist wohlgetan I*	?; 1:Rodigast 1674	5; 1; 0		W.Bn.	W.Bn. C, M	ICF		1731 or 1732
11/17	22 p. Trin.	55	*Ich armer Mensch, ich Sündenknecht*	?; 5: Rist 1642	5; 0; 1		W.Bn.	W.Bn. M, C	ICF	(Solo cant) : T	1731 or 1732

I Date	II Occasion	III BWV	IV Title	V Text	VI Mvts.	VII Score	VIII Pts. & Cop.	IX Wm.	X Remarks	XI Old Date
1726 *(cont.)*										
11/24	23 p. Trin.	52	*Falsche Welt, dir trau ich nicht*	?; 6: Reusner 1533	6 0 1(*)	W.Bn.	W.Bn. M, C	ICF	(Solo cant): S 1: cf. Brandenb. Conc. I/1	ca.1730
11/30	B'day:Prince Leopold's 2nd wife	(36a)	*Steigt freudig in die Luft*	Pic. (printed 1727)	9 (1)? 0				Cf. BWV 36c (1725), 36 (1731), & 36b (1735)	1726
12/1	1. Advent	?								
12/11	Inaug. of Lp. Univ. Prof. Kortte	207	*Vereinigte Zwietracht der wechselnden Saiten*	Pic.?	9(+1) 2 0	W.Bn.	W.Bn. C, JSB, etc.	ICF	Urform of 207a. 1,5: cf. Brandenb. Conc.I/3+4(Trio II)	1726

12/25 through 12/29 (Xmas—Sun.p.Xmas) :?

1726 or 1727

I Date	II Occasion	III BWV	IV Title	V Text	VI Mvts.	VII Score	VIII Pts. & Cop.	IX Wm.	X Remarks	XI Old Date
	Trin.	129?							See 6/16/1726	
?	?	204	*Ich bin in mir vergnügt*	Hunold 1713, enlarged by ?	8 0 0	E.Bn.		ICF	Sec. solo cant:S 8: cf. BWV 216/3	bef.1728

1727 *(Jahrgang IV, cont.)*

I Date	II Occasion	III BWV	IV Title	V Text	VI Mvts.	VII Score	VIII Pts. & Cop.	IX Wm.	X Remarks	XI Old Date
1/1	New Year?	225?	*Singet dem Herrn ein neues Lied* (Motet)	Ps.149, 150; ?; J.Gramann bef. 1539	1 or 3 1 or 3 0	W.Bn.	W.Bn. K4, M	ICF	More likely 5/12/1727: b'day of Elector of Saxony	1723-34 (or 1745/6)
1/5	Sun.p.New Year	58?	*Ach Gott, wie manches Herzeleid II* (Dialogus)	Moller 1587; 2-4: rev.by ?; 5:Behm 1610	5 0 0	W.Bn.	Lp. JSB, C etc.	ICF + MA (= 1733/4)	Solo cant:S.B. Reperf. 1733 or 34	1733

1/6 through 1/26 (Epiph.—3 p. Epiph.) :?

Date	Occasion	BWV	Title							Notes	Year
2/2	4 p. Epiph. (& Purification)	82	Ich habe genug	?	5 0 0		W.Bn. E.Bn. M etc.		ICF	Solo cant.:B (or S or Mezzo);2,3: cf. AMB Notebook, 1725; Nos. 34 and 38.	1731 or 1732
"	"	(83)?							Cont. ICF	Cf. 2/2/1724 Reperf.?	
2/6	Fun.Serv. for J.C.von Ponickau?	157?	Ich lasse dich nicht, du segnest mich denn	Pic.; 1: OT; 5: Keymann 1658	5 0 1					(Solo cant.):T,B. Also assigned to Purification. Sc & pts. cop'd by Penzel	1727
2/9	Septuagesima	84?	Ich bin vergnügt mit meinem Glücke	Pic., rev. by JSB?;5: AJvS-R 1686	5 0 1		E.Bn.		GAW+ S.CoA	(Solo cant.):S later orig. likely.	1731 or 1732
2/16 through 4/11 (Sexages.—Good Friday) : ?											
4/13	Easter	(232/ III)?	Sanctus in D (of the later B-minor Mass)				W.Bn. M, C, WF		4 pts.: S.CoA; 1 pt.: ICF	Or: 12/25/1726? Cf. 12/25/1724	
4/14 through 5/11 (2. Easter Day—Cantate Sunday) : ?											
5/12	B'day: August II	App.9	Entfernet euch, ihr heitern Sterne	C.F.Haupt	14 2? 0					Only text (Lp.1727) ext.	1727
"	"	225								See 1/1/1727	
5/18 through 6/8 (Rogate through Trinity—but cf. BWV 129: 6/16/1726!) : ?											

AFTER JAHRGANG IV, BUT STILL 1727

Date	Occasion	BWV	Title						Notes	Year
8/3	Name Day: August II	(193a)	Ihr Häuser des Himmels, ihr scheinenden Lichter	Pic.	11 2 0				Only text ext. Cf. Cö.: 1717-23 & 8/26/1726	1727
8/25	Inaug. of new Town Council	App.4	Wünschet Jerusalem Glück	Pic.; 1: Ps.122	6 1? 1				Only text ext. Reperf. & rev. 1730 and 1741	1727

I Date	II Occasion	III BWV	IV Title	V Text	VI Mvts.	VII Score	VIII Pts. & Cop.	IX Wm.	X Remarks	XI Old Date
1727 (cont.)										
8/31	12 p. Trin.	(69a)?					E.Bn. C	Mvt.3: MA	Cf. 8/15/1723	ca.1730
From 9/7 (13 p. Trin.) on: *Public mourning on account of death of Queen Christiane Eberhardine of Saxony and Poland.*										
10/17	Mem. Serv.: Queen & Electoress (at Univ. Church)	198	Lass, Fürstin, lass noch einen Strahl	Gottsched, 1727	10:7+3 / 3 / 0	E.Bn.		MA	1,3,5,8,10: cf. BWV 247 of 3/23/1731; 1,10 also: 244a/1+7	1727
1728										
2/5 (or 6/5)	Wedding: Wolff/ Hempel	216	Vergnügte Pleissenstadt	Pic.	7 / 0 / 0		2 pts: [Pr.?]		Sec. solo cant:S,A. S,A pts,once ext, now lost. 1,3,5,7 = 216a; 3:cf.204/8; 7: 205/13	1728
About 1728										
	2. Whits.	(173)				W.Bn. M		MA	Rev. of 5/29/1724(?) perf.; cf. also: Cö.	ca. 1730
	Inaug. of new Town Council	120?	Gott, man lobet dich in der Stille	Pic.?; 1: Ps. 65; 6: Luther 1529	6 / 1 / 1	NA		D. Eag.?	Or 1729?; 1,2,4: cf. 120a & b; Expecto of B-Mass & 1019a.	1728 (1730?)
	St. Michael	149	Man singet mit Freuden vom Sieg	Pic.; 1: Ps.118; 7:Schalling 1571	7 / 1 / 1(*)	Copy by Penzel, 1756		Horn	Or 1729 ?; 1: rev. of BWV 208/15	1731
	21 p. Trin.	188	Ich habe meine Zuversicht	Pic.; 6: Lübeck bef. 1603	6 / 0 / 1	[E.Bn.]		Horn	(Solo cant): S,A,T,B. 1: rev. of BWV 1052/3	1731
	Xmas Day	197a	Ehre sei Gott in der Höhe	Pic.; (1: NT); 7: K. Ziegler 1697	4 (7) / 0 (1) / 1	[Pr. N.Y.]		Horn + GAW	Music of 1-3 missing; (Solo cant): A,B 4,6 = 197/6 & 8.	1730-32

Date	Occasion	BWV	Title	Text	No.	Copyist/loc.	Instr.	Remarks	Year
3/24	Fun.Serv.: Prince Leopold of Cöthen	244a	*Klagt, Kinder, klagt es aller Welt*	Pic. (printed 1729); 8: Ps.68	24 / 6:2 id. / 0			Cf. BWV 198/1 +10; & BWV 244/ 10, 12, 47, 58, 66, 29, 26, 75, 19 + 78.	1728
4/15	Good Friday	244	St. Matthew Passion	Pic. 1729; NT and 13 hymns	78 / (21-26)? / 12 (?)			Sc. & pts. of this 1st perf. not ext.; cf. 244a: 10 mvts.	1729
4/18	2. Easter Day	VI	*Ich bin ein Pilgrim auf der Welt*	Pic.1729; 6: Stolshagen late 16th c.	6 / 0 / 1			(Solo cant); only 5 mm. ext. in aut. sc. of BWV 120a	
6/6	2. Whits.	174	*Ich liebe den Höchsten von ganzem Gemüte*	Pic.1728; 5: Schalling 1571	5 / 0 / 1	W.Bn.	Horn, + MA	(Solo cant) : A,T,B. 1 = Brandenb. Conc. No. III/1 rev'd	1729 orig.date
10/23	19 p. Trin.	App.2	?	?		[W.Bn. Pr.etc.] D, CPE[22], JSB etc.		Only 6 mm. & aut. heading ext.	
10/24	Fun.Serv.: Rector Ernesti	226	*Der Geist hilft unsrer Schwachheit auf* (Motet)	1(-3): NT; 4:Luther 1524	2 or 4 / 1 or 3 / 1	W.Bn. Krebs[23] CPE,AM	MA	Orig. date	1729
Presumably 1729									
1/1	New Year	171	*Gott, wie dein Name, so ist auch dein Ruhm*	Pic.1728; 1: Ps.48; 6: J.Herman 1593	6 / 1 / 1*	Pr. Switz.	Horn + GM?	1:4:6: cf. B-Mass (No. 13); BWV 205/9 & 41/6.	1730, completed after 1736
1/27	3 p. Epiph.	156	*Ich steh mit einem Fuss im Grabe*	Pic.1728/29; 2: Schein 1628; 6:Bienemann 1582	6 / 0 / 1	Lp.,but after 1750		1 = BWV 1056/2 rev'd. (Solo cant) :A,T,B	1729 or 1730

22. First appearance of Carl Philipp Emanuel Bach, just 15 years of age, as copyist of cantata parts.

23. Johann Ludwig Krebs's first appearance as copyist; from here on abbreviated: Kr.

I Date	II Occasion	III BWV	IV Title	V Text	VI Mvts.	VII Score	VIII Pts. & Cop.	IX Wm.	X Remarks	XI Old Date
Presumably **1729** *(cont.)*										
2/27	Estomihi	159	*Sehet, wir gehn hinauf gen Jerusalem*	Pic.1728/29; 1: NT; 2: Gerhardt 1656; 5: Stockmann 1633	5 0 1				(Solo cant) : A,T,B. Copy by Penzel	1727
4/19	3.Easter Day	145	*Ich lebe, mein Herze, zu deinem Ergötzen*	3-6:Pic.; 1: C. Neumann ca. 1700;2:NT; 7:N. Herman 1560	5(7) 0(1) 1(2)				1,2:by Telemann, added later; 3,5: of Cö. orig.?	1729 or 1730
?	Wedding	(120a)	*Herr Gott, Beherrscher aller Dinge*	? ; 8:J.Neander 1679	8:3+5 1(+1) 1(*)	[W. Bn.]	[E.Bn.] D, Kr.	GAW, CS, MA	Incomplete; 1,3,6: cf. 120/2,4,1; mvts. 4;8: BWV 29/1; 137/5	bef.1728 (or 1732/3?)
?	?	201	*Der Streit zwischen Phöbus und Pan (Geschwinde . . .)*	Pic.	15 2 0	W.Bn.	W.Bn. Kr., CPE	Horn, MA	7;15: cf. BWV 212/20; App.10/7 (= App. 19/9)?	1731
Perhaps also **1729**										
12/25	Xmas Day	(63)						CS	Cf. 12/10/1713? & 12/25/1723	
?	Wedding	250-252	3 Chorales	Rodigast 1674; J.J. Schütz 1675; Rinckart 1636	3 0 3		E.Bn. aut.	GAW	Dating based on watermark	?
1730										
4/7	Good Friday	246?	St. Luke Passion (not by JSB)	?		E.Bn. JSB + CPE		Horn		ca.1712

Date	Occasion	BWV	Title	Text source	Scoring	Material		Notes	Year
6/25	Jubilee of Augsburg Confession	(190)						Rev. of 1/1/1724 perf.	
6/26	2. Day of Jubilee	(120)						Cf.: About 1728	
6/27	3. Day of Jubilee	(App.4)						Cf. 8/25/1727	
8/25	Inaug. of new Town Council	App.3	Gott, gib dein Gerichte dem Könige	Pic.; 1: Ps.72	5 / 0 / (2?)	As above		Only text ext.	1730
9/17?	15 p. Trin.	51	Jauchzet Gott in allen Landen!	?; 4: Gramann (1548)	5 / 0 / 0	E.Bn.	W.Bn. Kr., etc.	MA; Solo cant.: S. 1729 or 1731 also possible	1731 or 1732
10/31?	Reformation	192?	Nun danket alle Gott	Rinckart 1636	3 / 2 / 0		[W.Bn.] Kr., etc.	MA; Incomplete	1731-34 (or 1746?)
1731									
2/2	Purification	(82)				Kr.		MA; Cf. 2/2/1727	
3/23	Good Friday	247	St. Mark Passion	Pic., printed 1732; NT; and 16(?) hymns	132 / 14? / 16?	Music lost, text ext.		5 mvts. survive in BWV 198; 2 in BWV 54/1 & 248/45.	1731

3/25 through 4/1 (**Easter—Quasimodogeniti**): reperf. of BWV 31, 66, 134 (rev'd) & 42.

Date	Occasion	BWV	Title	Text source	Scoring	Material		Notes	Year
4/8	Misericordia Domini	112?	Der Herr ist mein getreuer Hirt	W.Meuslin ca. 1530 (after Ps.23)	5 / 1 / 1(*)	NYPM Lp. D?		Horn, MA; Or 1729?	1731

4/15 through 5/20 (**Jubilate—Trin.**): reperf. of BWV 103, 37, 172, 173, 184, 194.

Date	Occasion	BWV	Title	Text source	Scoring	Material		Notes	Year
8/25	B'day: Count von Flemming	App.10	So kämpfet nur, ihr muntern Töne	Pic.1737	7 / 2? / 0			Cf. 1: Xmas Or. VI/1; 7: BWV 201/15. Only text ext.	

I Date	II Occasion	III BWV	IV Title	V Text	VI Mvts.	VII Score	VIII Pts. & Cop.	IX Wm.	X Remarks	XI Old Date
1731 (cont.)										
8/27	Inaug. of new Town Council	29	Wir danken dir, Gott, wir danken dir	? ; 8:Gramann 1548	8 / 1 / 1(*)	E.Bn.	W.Bn. Kr, CPE etc.	MA	1: cf. BWV 1006/1 & 120a/4; 2: cf. B-Mass/6+25	1731 aut.date
11/18	26 p. Trin.	(70)					2 pts: CPE+Kr.	MA	Reperf.; Cf. 11/21/1723	
11/25	27 p. Trin.	140	Wachet auf, ruft uns die Stimme	1,4,7: Nicolai 1599; 2,3,5,6: Pic.?	7 / 1		Lp. Kr, E, JSB, etc.	MA	4: cf. BWV 645, Schübler Organ Chorale No. 1	1731 (or 1742?)
12/2	1. Advent	36	Schwingt freudig euch empor	Pic.? or JSB ?; 2,6,8:Luther 1524; 4: Nicolai 1599	8:4+4 / 1 / 2	E.Bn.	W.Bn. Kr., etc.	MA	1,3,5,7: parody of BWV 36c (1725)	1728-36
1728-31										
Reperformances and/or revisions of BWV 110, 243 (Magnificat: D-major version), 151, 16, 23, 182, 245 (John Passion: 3rd version, 147, 79.										
?	?	117	Sei Lob und Ehr dem höchsten Gut	J.J.Schütz 1675	9 / 2 id. / 1	Pr. Switz.		MA		ca.1733
1732										
6/5	Consecr. of renovated St. Thomas School	App.18	Froher Tag, verlangte Stunden	J.H.Winckler	10:5+5 / 2 / 0				Only text ext.; Parody:App.12; 1,6: cf.BWV 11/1 & 233.	1732
7/6	4 p. Trin.	177	Ich ruf zu dir, Herr Jesu Christ	J. Agricola 1529?	5 / 1 / 1	E.Bn.	Lp. E	MA[24]	Aut. date	1732

					Mvts					
8/3	Name Day: August II	App.11	*Es lebe der König, der Vater im Lande*	Pic., printed 1737	11 / 1 / 0			Only text ext.	1. cf. B-Mass: Osanna + 215/1; 7: 248/IV/4 + 213/5; 9: BWV 30a/7	1732
1732-35										
	5 p. Trin.	(93)				Lp. E		MA	Cf. 7/9/1724	
1733										
4½ months of public mourning (from Estomihi to 4 p. Trin.): death of Augustus the Strong (Feb. 1), Elector and King of Saxony and Poland.										
?	Homage to new sovereign: August III	232/I	*Missa (Kyrie & Gloria of the later B-Mass)*		11 / 6 / 0	W.Bn. Dresd.	JSB, WF, CPE, AM	sc: MA, pts: unique	Date of dedication: 7/27/1733; Cf. BWV 191/1-3; 29/2 & 46/1	1733
8/3	Name Day: August III	(App. 12)	*Frohes Volk, vergnügte Sachsen*	Pic., printed 1737	11 / 2 / 0			Only text ext.	Parody of App.18, cf. 6/5/1732	1733
9/5	B'day: Prince Elector	213	*Hercules auf dem Scheidewege (Lasst uns sorgen . . .)*	Pic., printed 1737	13 / 2 / 0	E.Bn.	E, CPE, JSB,etc.	MA	Source of 6 mvts. of Xmas Or.; 5:= App. 11/7; 13: cf. BWV 184/6	1733
12/8	B'day: Electoress and Queen	214	*Tönet, ihr Pauken! Erschallet, Trompeten!*	?	9 / 2 / 0	E.Bn.	[E,Bn.] E, F	MA	Source of 4 mvts. of Xmas Or.	1733
1733 or 1734										
	Sun.p.New Year	(58)					AM + JSB	MA	Reperf. & rev. cf. 1/5/1727	

24. *MA* (italics) indicates the large size of the MA watermark.

I Date	II Occasion	III BWV	IV Title	V Text	VI Mvts.	VII Score	VIII Pts. & Cop.	IX Wm.	X Remarks	XI Old Date
1734										
2/19?	Coron. of August III (Jan.17)	(205a)	*Blast Lärmen, ihr Feinde! verstärket die Macht*	Pic.?	15 2 0				Parody of BWV 205; cf. 8/3/1725	1734
10/5	Annivers. of King's election	215	*Preise dein Glücke, gesegnetes Sachsen*	J.C.Clauder	9 2 0	E.Bn.	E.Bn. E,G,F, JSB,etc.	MA, D.Eag.	1: cf. App.11/1 + B-Mass (Osanna); 7: Xmas Or. V/5.	1734
10/24	18 p. Trin.	(96)							Reperf. & rev. cf. 10/8/1724	
11/21	Welcome to new Rector J.A.Ernesti	App.19	*Thomana sass annoch betrübt*	J.A.Landvogt	9 1 0				Only text ext. 9: cf. BWV 201/15 & App.10/7.	1734
?	?	97	*In allen meinen Taten*	P. Fleming 1642	9 1 1*	NYPL	E.Bn. Vg	MA, 1:ZVM	Aut. date	1734
11/28	1. Advent		Telemann's *Machet die Tore weit*			E.Bn.		ZVM	Aut.copy by JSB	
12/25/ 1734–1/6/ 1735	Xmas to Epiphany	248/ I-VI	Christmas Oratorio (= 6 cantatas)	Pic.? & JSB?; NT; Luther, Rist,Gerhardt etc.	65 10 2 id. 12(3*)	W.Bn.	W.Bn. G,E,F, etc.	sc:ZVM pts: MA	Aut.date: 1734. Much parody; cf. BWV 214, 213, 215, 247, App. 11 & 10.	1734
1735 *(cont.)*										
1/30	4 p. Epiph.	14	*Wär Gott nicht mit uns diese Zeit*	1,5:Luther 1524; 2-4: par. by ?	5 1 1	E.Bn.	Lp.+ E.Bn. AM, Vh	ZVM	Aut. date	1735

2/2; 4/11 & 4/12 (Purification; 2. & 3. Easter Day) : BWV 82; 66? (rev'd) & 134 (rev'd) reperformed.

Date	Occasion	BWV	Title	Text	No.	Score	Parts	Pub.	Notes	Year
5/19	Ascension	11	Lobet Gott in seinen Reichen (Ascension Or.)	?; 2,5,7,9: NT; 6: Rist 1641; 11: Sacer 1697	11 / 2 / 1	W.Bn.	NA	ZVM	1: cf.App.12/1 & 18/1; 4: Agnus Dei (B-Mass) + I/3; 10: I/5 (11/27/1725)	1730-40
8/3	Name Day: August III	(207a)	?Auf, schmetternde Töne der muntern Trompeten	Pic.?	9(+1) / 2 / 0		[W.Bn.] Vk,etc.	ZVM	Parody of BWV 207; cf. 12/11/1726	1734
About 1732—beginning of 1735										
?	6. p. Trin.	9	Es ist das Heil uns kommen her	1,7: Speratus 1523; 2-6: par. by ?	7 / 1 / 1	LC	Lp. AM, Ve	MA		1731
?	? (15 or 21 p. Trin.?)	100	Was Gott tut, das ist wohlgetan III	S. Rodigast 1674	6(or 1 2 1 *0)	E.Bn.	W.Bn. 2 sets: Vj,F,JSB	MA Z.I, D.Eag.	1,6: cf. BWV 99/1 & 75/7 (both re-orchestrated)	ca.1735 (bef.1733?)
?	?	211	Coffee Cantata: Schweigt stille, plaudert nicht	Pic.1732; 9, 10 added	10 / (1) / 0	E.Bn.	Vienna Vh, CPE[25]	MA	Solo cant.:S,T,B	ca.1732
Reperformances of BWV 62, 91, 41, 73, 249? (2nd version, now under the name "Oster-Oratorium"), 173, 129, 94, 5.										
1735? (7/28?)	Homage to Lp. U. Rector J.F. Rivinus	(36b)	Die Freude reget sich	Pic.?	8 / 2 / 0	E.Bn.	[E.Bn.] mostly JSB		Ornam. Parody & rev. of BWV 36c; cf. April or May, 1725	7/28/1733
1736										
3/30	Good Friday	(244)	St. Matthew Passion						Cf. 4/15/1729	
10/7	B'day: August III	206?	Schleicht, spielende Wellen, und murmelt gelinde	?	11 / 2 / 0	E.Bn.	E.Bn. JSB, Rider, GHB[26] etc.			1733

25. Philipp Emanuel's leaving of his father's house in the fall of 1734 becomes the *terminus ante quem* for the writing-out of the performing parts of the Coffee Cantata.

26. GHB = Bach's son, Gottfried Heinrich (1724-63). The extreme youth of the boy makes the attribution somewhat doubtful.

I Date	II Occasion	III BWV	IV Title	V Text	VI Mvts.	VII Score	VIII Pts. & Cop.	IX Wm.	X Remarks	XI Old Date
1736 or 1737										
?	Fun.Serv. (Motet)	118	O Jesu Christ, meins Lebens Licht	M. Behm 1608 (1611)	1 1 0	Pr. USA		Z+ NM, Rider	Re-orchestrated, cf. ca.1741-49	1740
1737										
9/28	Homage to J.C. von Hennicke	30a	Angenehmes Wiederau, freue dich . . .	Pic., 1737	13 2 id. 0	E.Bn.		Z+ NM	Uform of BWV 30; 1,5: cf. 195/ 8+6 (early version); 7:App.11/9; 11: 210/8	1737
About 1737										
?	?	233?	Missa in F		6 3 0	Only early 19th c. copies extant			4 mvts.:parodies; cf.BWV 102/3+5; 40/1 & (?) App. 18/6	ca. 1737
?	?	235?	Missa in G minor		6 3 0	"			All parody. Cf. BWV 102/1; 72/1; 187/4,3,5 & 1	ca. 1737
1738										
4/28	Homage to August III	App.13	Willkommen! ihr herrschenden Götter der Erden!	Gottsched	9 0? 0				Only text ext.	1738
1739										
8/31	Inaug. of new Town Council	(29)							Re-perf. Cf. 8/27/1731	
1736–about 1740										
	Good Friday	(244)	St. Matthew Passion						Version represented by the W.Bn.parts	

Date	BWV No.	Occasion	Incipit	Text	No. of movts	W.Bn.	E.Bn.	Copyist	Version represented by the beginning of the aut. score	Date
?	(245)	St. John Passion	" "							
?	30	St.John	Freue dich, erlöste Schar	Pic.?; 6: Olearius 1671	12: 6+6 / 2 id. / 1	W.Bn.	E.Bn. aut.	Z.II, Z+, NM	Parody of BWV 30a; cf. 9/28/1737	1738
?	240	?	Sanctus in G	?	1		E.Bn. ?	D.Eag.	Or bef. 1735? Authenticity doubtful	?
?	197	Church Wedding	Gott ist unsre Zuversicht	JSB?; 5:Luther 1524; 10: Neumark 1657	10: 5+5 / 1 / 2		E.Bn.	Z+, NM	6,8: cf. BWV 197a/4+6	1737 or 1738
?	210a	Homage to Count von Flemming (+2 other occasions)	O angenehme Melodei!	?	10 / 0 / 0		E.Bn.+[NA] Agricola	S.CoA	Solo cant.:S (only S.pt.ext.). Parod. in BWV 210. 8:cf.30a/11	1739 or earlier
1740										
8/29	V	Inaug. of new Town Council	Herrscher des Himmels, König der Ehren	? (Lp., 1740)	7 / 2? / 0				5,7:parod. of BWV 208/13 & 15	
1740 or 1742										
8/3	(208a)?	Name Day: August III	Same as 208	S.Franck, rev'd by ?	15 / (2) / 0				Cf.2/23/1713? + 4/19/1716. Parody of BWV 208	
1742										
8/30	212	Homage at Klein-Zschocher	Peasant Cantata: *Mer hahn en neue Oberkeet*	Pic., published 1751	24 / 0 / 0	W.Bn.		D.Eag.	Solo cant.:S.B;for C.H.von Dieskau. 20: cf. BWV 201/7	1742

Ca. 1741–49

I Date	II Occasion	III BWV	IV Title	V Text	VI Mvts.	VII Score	VIII Pts. & Cop.	IX Wm.	X Remarks	XI Old Date
12/25	Christmas Day	191	Gloria in excelsis Deo		3:1+2 2 0	E.Bn.		Eger	= *Gloria* of B-Mass, mvts. 1, 4 and 8 (4 & 8 rev'd). Cf. BWV 232/I:1733	ca.1740
?	Purification?	200	*Bekennen will ich seinen Namen*	?	1 0 0	[Pr.] Ln.		D.Eag.	Alto aria; fragm. of a lost cantata?	1735-49
?	1. Whits.	(34)	*O ewiges Feuer, o Ursprung der Liebe*	Weiss?, parod'd by JSB?	5 2 0	E.Bn.		Eger	Parody of BWV 34a. Cf. 3/6/1726	1740-41
9/11/1741?	Church Wedding: Naumburg Mayor/ Daughter of Pastor of Thomas' Church	195	*Dem Gerechten muss das Licht immer wieder aufgehen*	?; 1: Ps.97	8:5+3^{27} 3 0		4 pts: W.Bn. JSB etc.	D.Eag.	Early 8-mvt.version (rev.of 1728-31 work?); 6,8: cf. BWV 30a/5+1; See also: (ca. 1748?)	Urform: 1724? Rev.: ca.1730
?	?	234	Missa in A		6 3 0	Darm.	W.Bn. JCF?^{28}	Z.II, Lily	Parod. from BWV 67/6; 179/5; 79/2 & 136/1	ca. 1737/38
?	?	236	Missa in G		6 3 0	Darm.		Z.II	All parody: cf. BWV 179/1+3; 79/1+; 138/5 & 17/1	ca. 1737/38
?	?	(239)	Sanctus in D minor		1 1 0	E.Bn. aut.+ copy: H		Stag	Re-perf.(?) of an earlier (unauthentic?) work	?
?	?	(118)				Pr. Switz.		Eger	Re-orchestrated: ca. 1740-45; cf. 1736 or 1737	1740

Date	Event	(BWV)	Title / Text	Source	No.	Bn.		Notes	Year
?	Wedding	(210)	*O holder Tag, erwünschte Zeit*	?	10 / 0 / 0	E.Bn. some: JSB	S.CoA	Sec.solo cant:S. Parody of 210a: cf. 1736—about 1740. 8: cf. BWV 30a/11	ca. 1734/35
?	Inaug. of new Town Council (12 p. Trin.)	(69)	*Lobe den Herrn, meine Seele I*	?; 1: Ps.103; 6: Luther 1524	6 / 1 / 1*	E.Bn.		2 pts: Unicorn 49. 3rd version: 1743-49. Parody of 69a of 1723 & 1727.	1724
?	Good Friday	(244)	Performance of final version of St. Matthew Passion, based on the last (West Berlin) parts and (East Berlin) score.						
?	Good Friday	(245)	Performance of final version of St. John Passion, using the last set of the (East Berlin) parts of 1748/49.						
ca.1748²⁹		232/II-IV	Credo;Sanctus; Osanna to Dona nobis pacem(i.e. completion of B-Mass)		14 / 10 / 0	W.Bn. No pts.! (incl. 232/I)	From Credo on: Lily	Sanctus: cf. Xmas 1724. Parodies: BWV 171/1; 12/2; 120/2; App. 11/1+ 215/1; 11/4+ I/3; 29/2+232/I/6.	1733 (1734)
(ca. 1748?)	Wedding	(195)	See 9/11/1741 above! / ?; 1: Ps.97; 6: Gerhardt 1647		6:5+1 / 2 / 1(*)	E.Bn. H, JCF? JSB — W.Bn. JSB, H,Vr,AM	Lily	Sc. and pts. show late 6-mvt. version	
1749									
8/24	Inaug. of new Town Council	(29)	Re-performance, dated by text-print. Cf. 8/27/1731 and 8/31/1739. Last datable cantata performance in Bach's lifetime.						

27. The later—ca. 1748?—version substitutes a simple chorale for mvts. 6-8 (aria-recitative-chorus) the music of which is lost though 6 and 8 may survive in Cantata 30a/5 and 1.
28. Presumably Johann Christoph Friedrich Bach, born June 21, 1732.
29. Christoph Wolff's recent (1968) re-dating of the late portions of the B-minor Mass to the early 1740s is not borne out by graphological evidence.

Not datable at present
  BWV 143 *Lobe den Herrn, meine Seele* II
  BWV 158 *Der Friede sei mit dir* (3. Easter Day, 1725?)
  BWV 229 *Komm, Jesu, Komm!* (motet)
  BWV 230 *Lobet den Herrn, alle Heiden* (motet)
  BWV 242 Christe eleison in G minor

Bach's authorship doubtful
  BWV 203 *Amore traditore*
  BWV 209 *Non sa che sia dolore*

Not by J. S. Bach
  BWV 15   *Denn du wirst meine Seele nicht in der Hölle lassen* (by Johann
           Ludwig Bach)
  BWV 53   *Schlage doch, gewünschte Stunde* (by Georg Melchior Hoffmann)
  BWV 141 *Das ist je gewisslich wahr* (by Telemann)
  BWV 142 *Uns ist ein Kind geboren* (probably by Johann Kuhnau)
  BWV 160 *Ich weiss, dass mein Erlöser lebt* (by Telemann)
  BWV 189 *Meine Seele rühmt und preist* (by Georg Melchior Hoffmann)
  BWV 241 Sanctus in D (by Johann Kaspar Kerll)

Composer unknown
  BWV 237 Sanctus in C
  BWV 239 Sanctus in D minor
  BWV 240 Sanctus in G
  BWV 217-222 (5 church cantatas)

Fragments
  BWV 223 (lost)
  BWV 224
  BWV 231 BWV 28/2, but as *a cappella chorus* (included with choruses by
           Telemann and Harrer?). Cf. BWV App. 160.

The History and Dating of
Cantata No. 140

Wachet auf, ruft uns die Stimme was composed for the 27th Sunday after Trinity, a Sunday that occurs in the church year only when Easter falls extremely early. During the time of Bach's cantorate in Leipzig (1723-50), this happened just twice, in 1731 and 1742. Wilhelm Rust, in 1881, advocated the later date.[1] A year earlier, Spitta had come to the conclusion that 1731 was the correct year.[2] As the new chronology shows (p. 42), Cantata 140 was the next-to-last composition written on paper bearing the medium-sized MA watermark. This paper appears in Bach's compositions from October 1727 to December 2, 1731. Bach's favorite pupil, Johann Ludwig Krebs, who attended St. Thomas School from 1726 to 1735, has been identified as the principal copyist of the performing parts—the only surviving primary source, since the autograph score is lost. The use of this kind of paper and the presence of this particular handwriting serve as mutually reinforcing evidence that resolves any previous controversy over the date of Cantäta 140 in favor of the year 1731.

It might be worth recalling that Bach did not live at home when he composed Cantata 140. In 1731-32 the building that not only housed St. Thomas School and its pupils but also served as the living quarters of the rector and cantor was renovated and enlarged. Two new stories and a large mansard were added. Bach was to receive a new room in one of the upper stories and access to a private storage room in the attic. During the period of construction—from the end of June 1731 to April 21, 1732—

1. *BG XXVIII*, xxi.
2. Spitta, *op. cit.*, II, 459, 461, and 697.

Bach and his family found interim lodgings in the nearby house of a Dr. Christoph Donndorf. If Bach, frugal as he was, ate his midday meal at home, he had to walk four times daily from Donndorf's house in the Hainstrasse to the "school building where his *lectiones* were to continue, as well as conditions permitted."[3] Annoying and time-consuming as these circumstances must have been, they can hardly account for the apparent haste with which the parts of "Wachet auf" were written out by Krebs, Bach himself and four other copyists. At least any concrete evidence is lacking that would link Bach's living away from home with the state of the surviving performing parts of Cantata 140. In fact, it seems to have been Bach's habit to postpone the composition of his cantatas—even when, as in 1731, this was no longer a weekly task—until the score and performing parts were urgently needed.

* * *

When Bach died in 1750, his cantatas were divided between his two oldest sons. Wilhelm Friedemann, who as senior preserved the family tradition by becoming an organist, was even more out of step with his rationalistic age than his father had been. Maladjusted, he lost position after position and finally, in 1774, after ten years of unemployment, auctioned off the priceless treasure of his father's manuscripts. Among these was the autograph score of Cantata 140 which, along with that of Cantata 4 and many others, has since disappeared from view. Philipp Emanuel, on the other hand, kept his paternal legacy intact and passed it on to posterity.

It is fortunate that Anna Magdalena Bach was allowed to keep the performing parts (as distinct from the scores) of the so-called "chorale cantatas."[4] Bach's widow shared the fate of her husband's music; she too was forgotten. Not supported by her stepsons Friedemann and Philipp Emanuel, she was forced to offer these manuscripts to the city of Leipzig. In 1752, two years after her husband's death, she received 40 Thaler "because of her destitution, also (because) of some music turned over" by her.[5] For this poignant reason the original parts of 44 church cantatas have come down to us; they never left Leipzig, where they are still preserved.[6]

3. *Bach-Dokumente,* II (*Fremdschriftliche und gedruckte Dokumente zur Lebensgeschichte Johann Sebastian Bachs, 1685-1750*) , Kassel, Leipzig, 1969, p. 211.

4. Cf. p. 23 ff., Chronology, Jahrgang II.

5. Quoted by B. F. Richter, *Über die Schicksale der der Thomasschule zu Leipzig angehörenden Kantaten Joh. Seb. Bachs,* in *Bach-Jahrbuch,* 1906, p. 71.

6. They include Cantata 140, a microfilm of which was kindly put at my disposal by Dr. Alfred Dürr.

Bach's successor Gottlob Harrer (1750-55) seems not to have made use of these manuscripts. But shortly after Harrer's death, the interim conductor of the Thomas Choir, C. F. Penzel, made scores of 17 of them and, after he left Leipzig, of 7 more. Since Penzel copied some of these cantatas one or two weeks before the Sunday or holiday for which they were composed, church performances of them may well have occurred. Cantata 140 was the seventh among the 24 Penzel copied. However, the summer date on Penzel's score, August 10, 1755, speaks against a performance of this cantata, written for the 27th Sunday after Trinity. Penzel's copy later came into the possession of Felix Mendelssohn.

Another copy of the score of Cantata 140 supposedly derives from the estate of St. Thomas cantor J. F. Doles (1756-89), who is better known for keeping Bach's motets alive and for having introduced Mozart to Bach's eight-part motet *Singet dem Herrn ein neues Lied* in 1789. J. G. Schicht, the director of the Leipzig Gewandhaus concerts and editor of Bach's motets (1802/3), also copied some of Bach's cantatas—among them No. 140. Though we know that he performed Cantata 19, there is no proof that a performance of Cantata 140 actually took place.

Three years before the founding of the Bach Gesellschaft (BG), Cantata 140 was printed for the first time, in Carl von Winterfeld's *Der evangelische Kirchengesang*.[7] This quite faulty edition used a now-lost 19th-century source, made from Schicht's copy rather than from the original Leipzig parts. The final chorale of the cantata had already been published in the collections of Bach chorales that Philipp Emanuel Bach, J. P. Kirnberger, and C. F. Becker edited in 1769, 1785, 1831 and 1843. The Bach Gesellschaft published Cantata 140 in 1881 in its 28th volume, the last of nineteen edited by Wilhelm Rust. Rust resigned his editorship after the appearance (in 1880) of Spitta's Bach biography. The monumental work of the not-yet-39-year-old Spitta undermined— in one important respect wrongly[8]—views held by Rust throughout his long and fruitful editorship.[9] The later Eulenburg and Hänssler editions follow that of the *BG*.

From the beginning of the 19th century on, handwritten copies of Cantata 140 were ordered by at least nine eager Bach collectors outside of Leipzig. Fortunately, some of these copies used the original performing

---

7. Vol. III, Leipzig, 1847, pp. 172-219. Cf. below, p. 153, fn.

8. In the year after the completion of Spitta's biography, Rust seems to have perceived the crucial flaw in Spitta's chronology that was based on the watermarks in the paper of Bach's undated compositions. Rust assigned to two parts of Cantata 134—cf. *BG* XXVIII, xxvii—the Spitta-defying correct order by placing the 1st violin part with its "Halfmoon" watermark ahead of the "MA"-bearing continuo part.

9. Cf. *BG* XXVIII, xv f. and *BG* XLVI, xlvii f.

parts as their model; others were copied from the Penzel, Schicht, and (perhaps) Doles scores. Yet it would be wrong to conjecture an early performance history of Cantata 140 from the existence of the original parts, the many copies, and the two printings. Not even Mendelssohn, who revived Bach's *St. Matthew Passion*, seems to have performed the cantata of which he owned the earliest copy. By 1891—one hundred years after its founding—the Berlin *Singakademie* had given 60 performances of the *St. Matthew Passion*, 15 of the B-minor Mass, 8 of the Christmas Oratorio, 3 of the *St. John Passion*, as well as performances of several cantatas: 106 (28 times), 105 (5 times), 4 (4 times) and 104 (twice).[10] Cantata 140 was not in the repertory of Germany's most famous choral society. But it was the first Bach cantata performed in America. Although the first two festivals of the Bethlehem Bach Choir were devoted to performances of the B-minor Mass, the Christmas Oratorio and the *St. Matthew Passion*, the third festival in the Pennsylvania town opened on May 11, 1903, with *Wachet auf*.[11]

10. See Martin Blumner, *Geschichte der Sing-Akademie in Berlin*, Berlin, 1891; also Georg Schünemann, *Die Bachpflege der Berliner Singakademie*, in *Bach-Jahrbuch*, 1928, p. 138 ff.
11. Cf. Raymond Walters, *The Bethlehem Bach Choir*, Cambridge, 1923.

The History of the Hymn
and Its Melody

The opening, middle and last movements of Cantata 140 are based on the hymn text and melody, *Wachet auf, ruft uns die Stimme*, by Philipp Nicolai (1556-1608).

> The hymn is a reversed acrostic, the initial letters of its three stanzas, W. Z. G., standing for "Graf Zu Waldeck" (Count of Waldeck), Nicolai's former pupil who died in 1598, aged fifteen.[1] The hymn probably was written in 1597, during the pestilence in Unna in Westphalia where Nicolai then was a pastor.[2]

While 1,300 of Unna's inhabitants succumbed to the epidemic, Nicolai, expecting death himself, recorded his meditations. Having miraculously survived, he appended to the finished manuscript the two hymns, with their tunes, that were to assure for him some measure of immortality. He published the whole work under the name *Freudenspiegel des ewigen Lebens* (Mirror of joy of the eternal life) the following year (1599) in Frankfurt am Main.[3]

These two hymns became famous almost overnight. The many editions of the *Freudenspiegel*, and the early uses of the two hymn tunes by composers such as Praetorius and Scheidt, testify to this.

The poem *Wachet auf* . . . recalls the Minnesinger time of Wolfram

1. The initial letters of the seven stanzas of Nicolai's other great hymn, *Wie schön leuchtet der Morgenstern*, spell—in correct order—Wilhelm Ernst Graf Und Herr Zu Waldeck (Wilhelm Ernst Count and Lord of Waldeck).

2. C. S. Terry, *Bach's Chorals* [sic], 3 vols., London, 1915-21, II, p. 405.

3. See facsimile reprint, Soest, 1963, p. 409 ff. and 412 f. Cf. also W. S. Kelynack, *The Fourth Century of Philipp Nicolai*, in *The Choir*, XLVII (1956), 136.

von Eschenbach, particularly the Morning Song (*Tageweise*), in which the watchman on the battlement of the knight's castle breaks the quiet of the night with his horn call, warning the lovers that dawn approaches and they must part. These Morning Songs were still printed as broadsheets in the 16th century, the century that saw their transformation into sacred watchmen's songs. The last of them is Nicolai's magnificent hymn, which has been called the "King of Chorales." The warning call to the lovers became the watchmen's call to Zion. Nicolai subtitled his hymn: "Of the Voice at Midnight, and (of) the Wise Virgins, who meet their Heavenly Bridegroom. Matthew 25,"[4] thus describing precisely the portion of the Gospel (Matthew 25:1-7) that he selected for his hymn: the expectation of the Bridegroom, the ecstatic joy at his coming, and the union with him. The Foolish Virgins do not appear in his hymn.

Like Luther's *Christ lag in Todesbanden*,[5] so too is Nicolai's hymn tune assembled with great ingenuity from older melodic phrases. The sequence of composition recalls Meistersinger procedure: creation of a poem, borrowing of melodic fragments, and welding them into a new melodic whole that fits the poem. Nicolai, who has been called "the last Meistersinger,"[6] actually incorporated the phrase:

from Hans Sachs's famous *Silberweise* into his hymn tune. There it occurs, as in Sachs's melody, three times, as the final phrase of the two Stollen and the *Abgesang*. The first phrase of Nicolai's tune can be traced all the way back to the psalm tone of the Lydian (5th) church mode, e.g.:

Protestant usage of this melodic formula is verified by the Strasbourg Psalm melody of 1538.

Terry[7] calls attention to two other forerunners of Nicolai's opening

---

4. Cf. Ludwig Kurtze, *D. Philipp Nicolai's Leben und Lieder (Nach den Quellen)*, Halle, 1859, p. 126 ff.

5. See G. Herz, *op. cit.*, p. 26 f.

6. By Walter Blankenburg, *Die Kirchenliedweisen von Philipp Nicolai*, in *Musik und Kirche*, XXVI (1950), 173.

7. *Op. cit.*, II, 405-06.

phrase. The first is the German *Agnus Dei*, Nikolaus Decius' *O Lamm Gottes unschuldig* of 1542[8]:

The other is the beginning of *In dulci jubilo*,[9] in which, however, the melody is turned into triple meter:

The fact that Nicolai ends the last stanza of his hymn with the words "in dulci jubilo" proves that at least the latter melodic kinship is more than coincidence.

Structurally, Nicolai's tune is closely related to Strasbourg hymns and tunes, particularly to those of Matthias Greitter. Both of Nicolai's chorales share the large dimensions of their 12-line stanzas with Greitter's *Es sind doch selig alle die* (best known from Bach's use in the *St. Matthew Passion* as *O Mensch, bewein dein Sünde gross*). These hymn tunes have three vital characteristics in common: (1) the *Stollen* is composed of *three* phrases which are repeated, the *Abgesang* of six; (2) the first phrase of the *Abgesang* is repeated; and (3) the final phrase is a variant of—in the case of *Wachet auf*, even identical with—the closing phrase of the *Stollen*.

Greitter: $\|{:}\ a_1\ a_2\ a_3\ {:}\|{:}\ b_1\ {:}\|\ b_2\ b_3\ b_4\ a_3'$

Nicolai: $\|{:}\ a_1\ a_2\ a_3\ {:}\|{:}\ b_1\ {:}\|\ b_2\ b_3\ b_4\ a_3$ (*Wachet auf*)

　　　　　$\|{:}\ a_1\ a_2\ a_3\ {:}\|{:}\ b_1\ {:}\|\ b_2\ b_2\ b_2'\ a_3'$ (*Wie schön leuchtet*)

Luther's saying that "music instills life into the text" is borne out by Nicolai's picturesque way of underlining key words of the text through the music. This simple form of tone painting is, however, limited to the first stanza, in the case of *Wachet auf* even to its first *Stollen* (see p. 115). Though Nicolai's two tunes still represent the end of the century of the Reformation, they also point to the future, for they are written in the major tonality that has its origin in the 5th church mode.

8. This hymn tune itself goes back to the *Qui tollis* from the Agnus Dei of Gregorian Mass No. 17.

9. Cf. Fridolin Sicher's ms. organ tablature book, St. Gall, 1503-31.

THE SCORE OF
CANTATA NO. 140

ACKNOWLEDGMENT

This edition of Johann Sebastian Bach's Cantata for the 27th Sunday after Trinity, *Wachet auf, ruft uns die Stimme*, BWV 140, is printed by permission of Bärenreiter-Verlag Kassel-Basel-Paris-London from *Johann Sebastian Bach, Neue Ausgabe sämtlicher Werke, herausgegeben vom Johann-Sebastian-Bach-Institut Göttingen und vom Bach-Archiv Leipzig, Serie I, Band 27, 1968 (BA 5032): Kantaten zum 24. bis 27. Sonntag nach Trinitatis, herausgegeben von Alfred Dürr.*

INSTRUMENTATION

Horn (*Corno*)
Oboe I
Oboe II
Taille

Violino piccolo
Violin I
Violin II
Viola

Soprano
Alto
Tenor
Bass

Continuo (Bassoon, *Fagotto*)
Continuo (Violoncello)
Continuo (figured and
    transposed: Organ)

---

1. Since the Violino piccolo is tuned a minor third higher than the regular violin, Bach notated the music for this part a minor third lower, i.e. in C. It is transposed to concert pitch in this edition.

2. The organs in Bach's time were tuned about a whole tone higher than normal pitch. During his Leipzig years, Bach notated the organ part a whole tone lower, therefore. In this cantata in E♭ major, the figured continuo (organ) part was thus written in D♭ major, while the bassoon and unfigured continuo (i.e. cello) parts were written in E♭.

CANTATA No. 140

WACHET AUF, RUFT UNS DIE STIMME

1. Chorale

I: Chorale

I: Chorale

I: Chorale

2. Recitativo

Tenore

Er kommt, er kommt, der Bräut-gam kommt! Ihr Töch-ter Zi-ons, kommt her-aus, sein Aus-gang

Fagotto
Continuo
Organo (bez.) Org.

ei - let aus der Hö - he in eu - er Mut - ter Haus. Der Bräut'gam kommt, der ei - nem

Re - he und jun-gen Hir-sche gleich auf de-nen Hü-geln springt und euch das Mahl der Hoch-zeit bringt.

Wacht auf, er-mun-tert euch! den Bräut-gam zu emp-fan-gen! Dort, se-het, kommt er her-ge - gan-gen.

3. Aria Duetto

Wenn kömmst du, mein Heil, wenn
Wann kommst

Ich kom - me, dein Teil,

III: Aria Duetto

war - - - te mit bren-nen-dem Ö - le.

ich kom - me.

4. Chorale

Zi - on hört die Wäch - ter sin - gen, das
Herz tut ihr vor Freu - den sprin - gen, sie wa - chet
und steht ei - lend auf.

Ihr Freund kommt vom Him - mel präch - - tig,   von

Gna - den stark, von Wahr - heit mäch - - tig,   ihr Licht wird

hell, ihr— Stern geht auf.

Nun komm, du wer - te Kron,   Herr Je - su,

Got - tes Sohn!   Ho - si - an - - na!

Wir fol - gen all   zum

Freu - den - saal   und hal - ten mit das A - bend -

mahl.

5. Recitativo

So geh her-ein zu mir, du mir er - wähl-te Braut! Ich ha-be mich mit dir von

E -wig-keit ver-traut. Dich will ich auf mein Herz, auf mei-nen Arm gleich wie ein Sie-gel set-zen und

dein be-trüb - tes Aug er-göt-zen. Ver - giß, o See-le, nun die Angst, den Schmerz, den

du er-dul-den müs-sen; auf mei-ner Lin-ken sollst du ruhn, und mei-ne Rech-te soll dich küs-sen.

6. Aria Duetto

Da capo *dal segno*

7. Choral

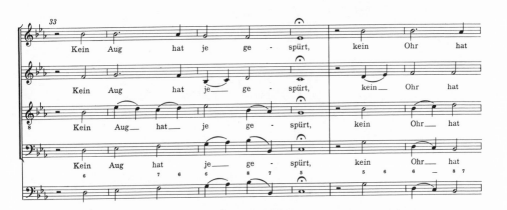

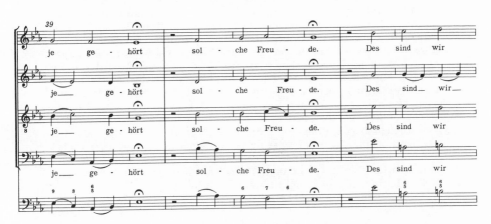

Textual Note

In contrast to BWV 4, the parts of Cantata 140 were not copied from an earlier autograph score, nor are there separate layers of parts attesting to performances at different times. The parts of BWV 140 seem to have been copied at great speed from the (probably) barely completed score. They are all written on the same paper, which bears the watermark MA in medium-size letters. In fact, the 57 pages needed for the parts of Cantata 140 reduced Bach's supply of this paper to the extent that a week later there was barely enough left for the copying of the parts of Cantata 36, written for the First Sunday of Advent. The uniformity of the paper shows clearly in the chart on p. 103.

Although Bach's autograph score is unfortunately lost, the parts tell their own story: a story of working against time to get the parts copied and the music rehearsed for November 25, the day on which the 27th Sunday after Trinity fell in 1731. If one considers the chart vertically as well as horizontally, one might conjecture as follows:

The grandiose opening chorale fantasy, which is (apart from the short closing chorale) the only movement employing all voices and instruments, contains at least one-half of the performance material of the whole cantata. With time at a premium, Bach may well have given his trusted disciple Krebs[1] the sheets on which he had just completed the composition of the first movement, so that Krebs could get a considerable head start on the time-consuming task of copying the cantata's 15 parts. Of these Krebs wrote out all but those for the first violin,[2] the bassoon and the transposed continuo (see chart, column 1: vertical direction). How many parts Krebs was able to complete by the time Bach finished his own composing labors, we shall never know. Either of the two following events may have occurred first: (1) if Bach were eager to get the parts into the hands of his soloists and choristers at the earliest possible moment, then Krebs would have completed the four vocal

1. Bach's testimonial on behalf of Krebs, written in 1735, shows how highly the composer thought of his student. See *The Bach Reader*, p. 135.

2. However, Dürr, in *Kritischer Bericht* to *NBA* I/27, p. 139, argues convincingly that Krebs also copied this now-lost part.

parts first (see chart: horizontal direction); (2) after this—or, less likely, before—Krebs wrote out the longest part, that of the continuo, which amounted to over 5 pages. From here on additional help could be employed. As a careful measure-by-measure comparison between Krebs's continuo and the bassoon part shows, the latter was copied exactly from the former by Copyist 4, not merely page by page, but—with only nine exceptions—line by line. When Bach realized that Copyist 4, like Krebs, would have to start a new page for the final chorale, the composer dashed it off himself, adding the designation "Bassono" on the blank first page.

At the same time another assistant, Copyist 5, prepared—from Bach's

WATER-MARK	MOVEMENTS: FORMS:	1 Chorus	2 Rec.	3 Duet	4 Chorus	5 Rec.	6 Duet	7 Chorale
	Soprano	Kr.		Kr.			Kr.	Kr.
	Alto	Kr.						Kr.
	Tenor	Kr.	Kr.		Kr.			Kr.
	Bass	Kr.		Kr.		Kr.	Kr.	Kr.
	Corno	Kr.						JSB
	Oboe I	Kr.					Kr.+ JSB*	Kr.
"MA" (medium size letters)	Oboe II	Kr.						Kr.?
	Taille	Kr.						Kr.
	Violino piccolo	Kr.		Kr.		JSB		JSB
	Violin I	E			E	E		E
	Violin II	Kr.			3	Kr.		Kr.
	Viola	Kr.			3	3+Kr.		JSB+ title: Viola
	Continuo	Kr.	Kr.	Kr.	Kr.	Kr.	Kr.	Kr.
	Bassoon	4	4	4	4	4	4	JSB+ title: Bassono
	Continuo (transposed)	5 Fig.: JSB	5 Fig.: JSB	5 Fig.: JSB	5 Fig.: JSB	5 Fig.: JSB	5 Fig.: JSB	5 Fig.: JSB

Abbreviations: Kr. Johann Ludwig Krebs.

JSB J. S. Bach, autograph.

E principal copyist E.

3, 4, 5 three further anonymous copyists to whom assignments were given. Their handwriting has not been traced in parts of any other cantatas.

Fig: *JSB* means that Bach added the figuring to the transposed continuo part.

* Krebs copied through m. 46; J. S. Bach from m. 47 on. Bach also added *piano* and *forte*—6 times—in lines 1-11. There are further autograph corrections and revisions, not mentioned in the above chart, in the following parts: S, B, Va., Cont. (non-figured) and Bassoon.

autograph score, or from Krebs's continuo, or even from the bassoon part—the part for the organ, which had to be transposed down a whole tone because the organs in Bach's time were tuned about a whole tone higher than the string and wind instruments. The transposed continuo part shows a mature hand—perhaps that of one of Bach's organ pupils—who copied apparently at breakneck speed what became the longest of all the parts, over 6 pages. Bach himself added the numbers for the figured bass. While frantic speed radiates from every measure of this part, Copyist 5 (adopting an idiosyncrasy of his time) was most generous when it came to the flats of his Db-major part. In grape-like clusters they decorate the beginning of each staff:

Copyist E, who later was to succeed Krebs as Bach's principal scribe from 1732-34, copied the first violin part with beautiful and harmonious penmanship. His model was most probably a now-missing violin part written by Krebs, since there were usually two such parts in a complete set, the first one made by the principal copyist and the duplicate by an assistant. Krebs and Copyist E were thus entrusted with the first copying of the glorious tune in the 4th movement that was destined to become the most popular melody from this cantata and one of the most beloved among all of Bach's melodies. The desire to have this tune properly phrased later led to countless additional slurs, which can be distinguished in the original parts by their blacker ink. Most of them make musical sense, but they crowd the part unnecessarily and distort the originally lean and clean score. Dürr demonstrated[3] that they are not by Bach and in the NBA edition of 1968 (reprinted here) presents for the first time Bach's score in its original form of 1731.

As this tune is scored for the two violins and viola in unison and time was of the essence, another scribe could now be pressed into service. His simple task was to copy the first violin part of the fourth movement into the second violin and viola parts. This occasionally somewhat slovenly scribe (Copyist 3) presumably worked from Krebs's now-lost first violin part. Then Copyist 3 decided to do more than he was supposed to. He copied the subsequent recitative (movement 5) from his model, not realizing that thereby he bestowed the first violin part upon the viola player. Krebs caught this mistake, scratched out these two wrong lines (with what good Saxon oaths we can only imagine), and wrote out the correct viola recitative himself. Bach then seems to have been drawn into this squabble; apparently having noted at the same time the waste of those two lines of staff, he took the part away from Krebs and wrote out the final chorale himself, squeezing it onto this page only by the

3. Dürr (*ibid.*, p. 131 f.) gives a complete account of these additions; an abundance of slurs in the obbligato parts of movement 4, some in movement 3 and a few in movement 6.

addition of a hand-drawn staff at the very bottom to accommodate the last 6½ measures. While all these activities were going on (apparently simultaneously and in the same room), Krebs must have tried to complete as many of his parts as possible.

In two cases Krebs's speed seems not to have been sufficient to suit Bach. In the *violino piccolo* part Bach himself took over, writing out the last two movements (5 and 7) himself, after Krebs had completed the highly ornate and long solo part of the first duet. In the second duet (movement 6) Bach did not even wait for Krebs to finish the solo oboe part. From the oblique direction of the first 4 notes of the second half of the duet, one can almost see Bach standing over Krebs; they look as if Bach had reached over, moving in on Krebs from the left. Bach's obvious hurry did not, however, interfere with his sense of economy. Again Bach added a full new staff as bottom line, but then got entangled in his own speed. He omitted a full measure—but caught the mistake almost immediately, for he restored it as the last measure of the same staff, indicating its proper place by a special insert symbol. After completing this movement, Bach let Krebs copy out the final chorale. Conceivably towards the end of this race for completion of the parts, Bach took even the simple one-page horn part from Krebs and wrote the necessary *tacet*[4] information and the final chorale himself. Thereby Bach saved no more than two minutes of time. Yet he must have considered them worth the effort towards the immediate goal of getting rehearsals of the full vocal and instrumental ensemble underway.

* * *

According to the practice of the *Neue Bach-Ausgabe*, editorial additions to the score are distinguished by the following means:

Letters (e.g. dynamic signs) and words in italics;
Phrasings in dotted lines;
Special signs (e.g. ornaments) in small print;
Accidentals (except those necessary to conform with modern practice) in small print.

Full details of the sources and their discrepancies will be found in Dürr's *Kritischer Bericht*.

4. Bach advises the horn player that he "is silent" (*tacet*) during movements 2 through 6.

ANALYSIS

The Chorale Melody as Used by Bach

Comparison between Nicolai's tune and Bach's use of it reveals the typical rhythmic changes most old hymn tunes underwent in the course of time. With regard to *Wachet auf* we can follow them from Jakob Praetorius's setting of 1604[1] to Bach's own time.

Wachet auf (Praetorius, 1604)

Wachet auf (Bach, 1731)

Bach changes the melody less than Buxtehude does in the highly ornate version of his cantata of 1687 (?)[2]; and he changes it no more than the latter's father-in-law Tunder who, while embellishing the cantus firmus, alters only its second phrase, a_2.[3] This is precisely the phrase Bach

1. Cf. Kurtze, *op. cit.*, p. 131 f.
2. *Buxtehudes Werke*, VI, Hamburg 1925 ff. One of Buxtehude's cantatas on this chorale is now readily available in America: Concordia, St. Louis, 1966.
3. Max Seiffert (ed.), *Organum*, 1. Reihe, No. 13, Leipzig, n.d.

changes, too, though more radically (see example). Except for this and the omission of the "warble" at the end of the first phrase, a_1, Bach leaves Nicolai's tune intact.

In contrast to Luther's Dorian and basically diatonic *Christ lag in Todesbanden,* Nicolai's tune, in the bright tonality of F, draws its inspiration from the fanfare-like rising triad which gives a_1 its distinctive character. Climbing then to the chorale's melodic peak, it outlines the six-four chord[4] in a_2. But while a_1 rises from the bottom note to the fifth, a_2 moves from fifth to the principal tonality and back to the fifth. Hans Sachs's phrase, a_3, with its characteristic leaps of several fourths, finally returns to the bottom note from which the tune had risen. The five phrases of the *Abgesang* (B),[5] which precede the eventual return of a_3, are considerably shorter and, above all, diatonic; two descend, and one rises from fifth to tonic while two others rise and then descend.

The Remainder of the Text and the Overall Form of the Cantata

Between the three stanzas of Nicolai's hymn, an unknown 18th century poet (perhaps Picander) inserted two rhymed recitatives, each followed by a poem which Bach called "Aria." These arias are, however, true duets—dialogues between Jesus and the Soul—the first yearning, the second a pure love duet. They give an indication of the kind of music Bach might have composed in abundance had his Elector and King responded in 1733 to Bach's request and appointed him composer to the Saxon Court.

The two love lyrics are characteristic of the Pietistic trend of the

4. The author realizes that he anticipates here a term that applies to the harmonic version rather than the original monodic hymn tune.

5. The terms *Stollen* and *Abgesang* derive from the *Bar* form (A-A-B) of the Meistersinger and Minnesinger songs (cf. Kothner's and Hans Sachs's explanations in Wagner's *Die Meistersinger*). Most Protestant chorales follow the pattern of *Bar* form. The *Stollen* is the first section, of two or three musical phrases, which is repeated to a rhyming text. The *Abgesang* is the concluding section, and tends to consist of twice as many phrases (although often shorter ones) as make up the *Stollen*.

18th century, which encouraged the individual soul to address itself directly to its Savior. When Spitta encountered such a "charming love duet" between Jesus and the Soul for the first time in Cantata 21[6], he seemed almost embarrassed by its all-too-personal style. Though he detected a "mitigating circumstance" in the fact that the soprano part was sung by a boy, Spitta admitted some justification in the reproach brought often against Bach by his time that his church music contained "theatrical and pietistic elements."

The love motive of the duets in Cantata 140 caused their poet to ← turn to the greatest love song of the Bible as a source of inspiration: the Song of Solomon. From it he quotes and paraphrases—more to *his* heart's content than to ours. In fact, his versification is at times quite insipid. Although Bach's score fails to name the two roles as such, the last line of the first duet: "Come Jesus!"—"Come, lovely Soul!" leaves no doubt as to their identity. The choice of the voices may be both symbolic and dictated by tradition. Thus the tenor as narrator (in the first recitative), the soprano as the Soul, and the bass as the voice of Christ (in movements 3, 5, and 6) follow a time-honored convention.

While the chart on p. 112 summarizes the textual significance of each movement, its chief purpose is to demonstrate that the overall form of a Bach composition is a beautifully proportioned and superbly organized whole. The design of BWV 140 is *chiastic*,[7] the 4th movement (the arrival of the Bridegroom) being its axis.

The three hymn stanzas represent the congregation by their use of the hymn text, by their collective choral sound, and by the common hold they have on the tonic key of E♭ major (itself conceivably chosen for the symbolic implication of its three flats). The interpolated pairs of recita- ← tives and duets depict the individual by the intimate and personal lyrics of their 18th-century poet, by the use of solo voices, and by the shifting of the harmony to neighboring keys. The result of this juxtaposition is an impressive contrast between the sturdy chorale stanzas and the subjective, at times almost romantic, emotions of pleading and uninhibited rejoicing in the solo movements.

6. Spitta, *op. cit.*, I, pp. 537-38. Other such love duets occur in cantatas 172, 152, 32, 49, and 145.

7. This type of form goes back to the Greek letter *chi* (X), which signifies the name of Christ by its initial letter and also by its shape as a cross. The over-all design of a chiastic composition groups pairs of movements symmetrically around a central movement. The latter functions as an axis or as a vertical mirror that catches, reflects, and thus relates the movements to each other like mirror images. Cf. Herz, *op. cit.*, pp. 84-86.

MOVEMENTS	1	2	3	4	5	6	7
TEXT AUTHORS	Nicolai: stanza 1	Unknown poet	Unknown poet	Nicolai: stanza 2	Unknown poet	Unknown poet	Nicolai: stanza 3
FORMS	Chorale Fantasy	Recitative	Duet	Unison Chorale	Recitative	Duet	Chorale
VOICES AND ORCHESTRATION	All voices and full orchestra	Tenor and Cont.	S and B, Vn.-picc. and Cont.	Tenor, Strings, Cont.	Bass, Strings, Cont.	S and B, Oboe and Cont.	All voices and full orchestra
KEYS	E♭ (T)	c (Rm)	c (Rm)	E♭ (T)	E♭ to B♭ (T to D)	B♭ (D)	E♭ (T)
CONTENT	The watchmen awaken the faithful	Heralding of the arrival of the Bridegroom	The Soul's yearning vs. Christ's words of comfort	The arrival	Christ's acceptance of the Bride	Bliss of union	Thanksgiving

T = Tonic;   D = Dominant;   Rm = Relative minor.

Movement I

Nicolai: Stanza 1

Ob. I, II; Taille;
Vi. piccolo with Vn. I;
Vn. II; Va.; Cont.
S (c.f.; doubled by Corno) ;
A, T, B

3/4; E♭ major
Chorale fantasy
Bar form, framed by ritornel

CHORALE PHRASE		TEXT LINE		
A	a₁	1	Wachet auf, ruft uns die Stimme	"Awake," the voice of watchmen
	a₂	2	Der Wächter sehr hoch auf der Zinne,	calls us from high on the tower,
	a₃	3	Wach auf, du Stadt Jerusalem!	"awake, you town Jerusalem!"
A	a₁	4	Mitternacht heisst diese Stunde;	Midnight is this (very) hour;
	a₂	5	Sie rufen uns mit hellem Munde:	they call to us with bright voices:
	a₃	6	Wo seid ihr klugen Jungfrauen?	"where are you, wise virgins?
B	b₁	7	Wohl auf, der Bräutgam kömmt,	Take cheer, the Bridegroom comes,
	b₁	8	Steht auf, die Lampen nehmt!	arise, take up your lamps!
	b₂	9	Alleluja!	Alleluja!
	b₃	10	Macht euch bereit	Prepare yourselves
	b₄	11	Zu der Hochzeit,	for the wedding,
	a₃	12	Ihr müsset ihm entgegengehn!	you must go forth to meet him."

Rhyme scheme (somewhat less regular than in stanzas 2 and 3) :
a a' b - c c b' - d d' e f f g (or b")
Metric scheme (alike in all 3 stanzas) : a b b' - a b b' - c c d d d b'

→*Wachet auf, ruft uns die Stimme* is one of Bach's later cantatas,[8] and every one of its seven movements is original in concept throughout.[9] Stylistically it could almost be one of the chorale cantatas of *Jahrgang* II (1724-25), at least as far as its two outer movements are concerned: the magnificent opening chorale fantasy, based on the first stanza of Nicolai's hymn, and the simple 4-part chorale harmonization at the conclusion of the cantata, using Nicolai's third and last stanza. But in 1724 Bach would have used paraphrases of Nicolai's second stanza as text for his recitatives and arias (or duets) in the middle movements. We may be grateful that in the year 1724 no 27th Sunday after Trinity occurred; for in 1731 Bach gave us the glorious unison chorale based on the unaltered text of that second stanza (movement 4), as well as the connecting recitatives and duets using newly written texts. The first movement is a chorale fantasy on the grandest scale, scored for all the instruments and voices Bach employs in this cantata.

Fifteen months before he composed Cantata 140, in his *Short but most necessary Draft for a well-appointed Church Music* ... (August 23, 1730), Bach lists the necessary position of "3rd Hautbois" or "Taille" player as "vacant." We know that university students or alumni of the Thomas School used to fill in for the missing regular musicians that Bach requested so often in vain. In slightly more than half of the 32 church cantatas in which Bach uses three oboe parts,[10] he requires the *taille* instead of a 3rd oboe. He notates the *taille*, his tenor oboe, in the alto clef, and frequently lets it double the viola, calling upon both instruments to strengthen the tenor voice in the concluding chorale. When Bach uses the *taille* for one or two obbligato parts rather than as tenor of a 3-part oboe choir, he refers to the instrument as *oboe da caccia*.[11] But usually he incorporates this independent and more elaborate *oboe da caccia* music into the first (and second) oboe part(s), thereby assigning its execution to his more skillful oboe player(s). *Taille* and *oboe da*

8. Only the following 12 church cantatas are, according to the new chronology, later: BWV (36), 177, 97, 14, [11] (the Ascension Oratorio), 9, [100], 118 (really a short one-movement motet), 30, [197], (191), and 195. But only half of them are newly composed. While those in brackets have only a few parodied movements, those in parentheses are mostly or all parody.

9. There are no adaptations (parodies) from earlier compositions in Cantata 140, though its 4th movement was transcribed later (in 1746 or 47) as a chorale-prelude for organ.

10. Cantata 31 uses four: 3 oboes and a *taille*.

11. For the use of *taille* and *oboe da caccia* in one and the same composition, see Cantatas 101 and 186.

caccia are both tuned a fifth lower (f-g²) than the oboe and are thus forerunners of the modern English horn. The *oboe da caccia* was curved or sickle-shaped, with a pear-shaped bell, while the *taille* had a straight tube and an open bell. We may suppose that Bach made no such distinction; he was probably glad enough just to locate· a capable player with an instrument of the proper pitch, be it straight or curved!

The *violino piccolo* is best known from Bach's First Brandenburg Concerto. While in Cantatas 96/1 and 102/5 it appears only as an alternate instrument to the *flauto piccolo* or *flauto traverso*, it plays a prominent obbligato role in Cantata 140. Leopold Mozart[12] associated the shrill sound of the violino piccolo with nocturnal music. Did Bach too think of this traditional association when he employed the "three-quarter violin tuned a minor third higher,[13] and sharper in tone than the usual violin"[14] for his nocturnal Cantata 140?

Bach used the *corno* (or *corno da caccia*) on many ocasions in support of the choral sopranos. Since the instrument was played by trumpet players "apparently on trumpet-like mouthpieces, and held bell up . . . the effect was . . . gayer and brisker"[15] than that of its modern counterpart, the French horn. A separate part written out for the bassoon enables the reeds in Cantata 140 to meet the strings on equal terms.

As is his custom, Bach entrusts the hymn tune unadorned and in long note values to the sopranos, and, for additional strength and color, to a horn—the watchman's instrument. The perfect matching of words and tune in the first *Stollen* is Nicolai's characteristic contribution to the history of the chorale. Here the opening rising major triad portrays the watchmen's call, "Awake!" The tune then rises with the words "*high* on the tower" to its melodic peak, a_2. Did Nicolai also make use of the musically necessary return to the tonic to depict, with the following descending line a_3, the "town Jerusalem" which in midnight darkness (text line 4) lies asleep below the watchmen's tower?[16] When the next three lines (4-6) are repeated to the same tune, the previous ideal relationship between word and music is of necessity disturbed. In the *Abgesang* it never existed.

12. Leopold Mozart, *Versuch einer gründlichen Violinschule*, Augsburg, 1756, 2nd ed., 1770, p. 2.

13. The part is notated a minor third lower, i.e., in C.

14. Curt Sachs, *Our Musical Heritage*, New York, 1955, p. 222.

15. *Ibid.*, p. 223.

16. So Friedrich Smend believes. *Johann Sebastian Bach: Kirchen-Kantaten*, Berlin, (3rd ed.) 1966; fascicle IV, p. 43.

This *cantus prius factus* Bach uses, along with its text, as the golden thread for his majestic tonal picture. For this the orchestra serves as frame as well as backdrop; unlike the voices, it is ever present. It opens and closes the movement with a festive ritornel that returns in the form of varied interludes to keep the vocal sections neatly separated. But the orchestra is also the constant and enlivening background for the vocal portions themselves. During much of the movement the upper-string and double-reed choirs are treated, measure for measure, in alternation. Dotted rhythms, syncopations, and wave after wave of sixteenth notes keep the thematic material of the instruments distinctly apart from that of the voices. Bach calls upon his chamber orchestra to supply the instrumental idiom that transcends the natural limitations of the human voice.

The thematic material of the instruments is contained fully in the 16-measure ritornel. (As the symbols a_1-a_3 and b_1-b_4 are already called upon to designate the different chorale phrases, we shall use x, y, and z to denote the motifs that make up the orchestral ritornel.) Alternating strings and oboes hammer out the incisive dotted rhythm of the French overture, x, which creates the sensation of a festive march and which, through the power of its melodic rise, seems to move relentlessly onward (mm. 1-4). It is as though Bach was inspired by the stanza's last line: "You must go forth to meet him." Smend[17] might go too far when he hears the 12 strokes of the clock at midnight in the rhythmic beats of these answering chords (see example), which recur throughout the movement. Yet there are 12 beats and the text does say in line 4: "Midnight is this (very) hour." Melodic rise and bar-by-bar alternation—now between

1st violin and 1st oboe, overlapping one another—continue with motif y. Rhythmically twisting and melodically unsure of its ascent, y counteracts the processional forward movement of x by its to-and-fro movement (mm. 5-8). At the same time motif y has the important melodic function of anticipating the triadic opening of the first chorale phrase. The bass reinforces its melodic outline one beat later in the dotted rhythm of x and serves as a sturdy antidote to the faltering steps of y.

17. *Ibid.*

With *z* (mm. 9-15; see example) the violins stabilize their former syncopated rhythm to five straight ascending surges of sixteenth notes. Against these the first oboe descends quietly in long sustained steps that seem to anticipate the opening chorale phrase of the *Abgesang*, b_1, before joining the violins in quasi-parallel motion in the last two bars (mm. 14-15). In a final measure (16) all instruments unite in a vigorous

homorhythmic tonic cadence, climaxing the motion that has steadily increased from *x* through *y* to *z*.

On the final cadential chord the sopranos enter with the first phrase of Nicolai's hymn tune, a_1. It is heard upon the background of motifs *x* and thinned-out *y*. To assure that the center of activity shifts audibly to the cantus-firmus voice, Bach marks the throbbing rhythm, *x*, in the orchestra piano (mm. 17-18). This accomplished, he allows its continuation (*y*, m. 19 ff.) to return to forte. But, mindful of the vocal activity that now begins to unfold, Bach deprives *y* of its former overlappings and of the supporting staccato chords by Vn. II, Va., Ob. II, and Taille. Once the triadic call of the watchmen has been sounded by the sopranos, Bach calls upon his choral altos, tenors, and basses as a third and all-important dramatic force to implement his tonal picture. Since the chorale melody, by its very nature as a traditional cantus firmus, cannot supply comment, it now behooves the three other voices to add a subjective element, to supply psychological insights and picturesque or dramatic detail.

This is not a Pachelbel-type chorale fantasy. Hence there will be no fugal anticipation of the chorale phrases by the accompanying voices. They follow rather than anticipate the soprano's cantus-firmus phrases. Their task is to cheer the cantus-firmus tune, phrase by phrase, along its predestined course in the treble. Their vocal comments change with each different chorale phrase (being alike only when the chorale repeats itself). The accompanying voices are lively, psychologically apt—and, at one point (b_2), even impatient with the slow pace of the hymn tune. To each of its sustained notes they tend to add six eighth notes of their own. This establishes the following rhythmic relationship: S (cantus firmus) : dotted half notes; other voices: eighth notes; orchestra: sixteenth notes or the dotted rhythm of x; and continuo: predominantly three staccato chords per measure. The accompanying voices will do most of their energetic urging-on in carefully-spaced bursts of fervor. As if this were a mass scene on the theater stage, Bach changes the order of their mostly imitative entrances as often as possible.

In a_1, the altos echo the sopranos' call "Wachet auf" with their own faster, embellished version of that call which is then taken up by tenors and basses (see example). A brief orchestral interlude, based on x in B♭

mm. 17-22

major, separates a_1 from a_2. When the sopranos enter with a_2 ("the watchmen call *high* on the tower"), the other voices can hardly wait to scale, with even greater speed, the peak of their own ranges, which they also reach on the word "high." One by one they do this again (T, A, B, and even continuo), each eager to urge the sopranos on in the right

mm. 29-34

upward direction (see example). While at a_1 the other voices wait until the sopranos have sung their third cantus-firmus tone before chiming in with commentary, at a_2 they intervene after the second cantus-firmus note. When a_3 is due, after an orchestral interlude based on a variant of y, the three lower voices not only crash in together but also simultaneously with the cantus-firmus-carrying sopranos (m. 43). It is as though Bach intended to rouse the town with the staccato quarter-note shouts of "Wach auf" and the ensuing eighth-note leaps on the same words. At the same time, the orchestral motifs x and y, adapted to the harmony of the voices, overlap the seven last measures of a_3.

The ritornel, living up to its name, is now repeated and the whole of A is heard again, sung to text lines 4, 5, and 6. While 4 and 5 lack any intimate connection between text and tune, line 6, with its repeated, impatient question "wo, wo?" (where, where?), at least does not run counter to the text. The ritornel separating A and B consists only of y and z, with y being subjected to melodic and harmonic changes before z takes over and completes the ritornel in the dominant B♭ major. Bach portrays the increasing animation implied in the text ("Take cheer, the Bridegroom comes") by letting bass, tenor, and alto enter now with their excited syllabic shouts before the sopranos intone chorale phrase b_1.[18] After a return of x, this process is repeated. Here, at the repeat of b_1, Bach's upward-leaping contrapuntal voices counteract the incongruity between the energetic exhortations of the text ("arise, take up your lamps!") and the placidly descending cantus-firmus phrase (m. 127 ff.).

The *alleluja* is to Bach the logical peak of excitement. He betrays his dissatisfaction with the four calm, diatonic notes of Nicolai's cantus-firmus phrase, b_2, by allowing his altos, tenors, and basses to express the *alleluja* spirit on their own—the way he understood it, as fervent jubilation. In Bach's melismatic abandon (m. 135 ff.), something lives on of the spirit of the medieval *alleluja*, with its exuberant vocalization on the last syllable, the *jubilus*. For 14 measures Bach's voices have a magnificent little triple fugato of their own. Entering in the following order: alto (G minor), tenor (B♭ major), and bass (E♭ major), they exult on a 4-measure subject (1) abounding in sixteenth notes, which is combined with two countersubjects (2 and 3; see chart below). Since the cross rhythm of the second measure of subject 1 (mm. 137, 141, 145) is remi-

---

18. With somnambulistic assurance Bach had in the *Stollen* narrowed the gap between cantus firmus and entrance of the accompanying voices from 2 1/3 measures at a_1, to 1 1/6 measures at a_2, to nothing at a_3. Now the accompanying voices even move ahead of the cantus firmus phrase b_1 (by 5/6th of a measure).

niscent of *y*, it constitutes an intrusion of the instrumental into the vocal realm. Up to this point Bach had kept these two spheres articulate and separate, but in the *alleluja* excitement their boundaries become blurred. When the sopranos finally enter—anticlimactically, we will have to admit—with their modest 4-note cantus-firmus phrase (b₂), it appears as no more than a whitecap carried by a rolling wave. In fact (in mm. 151-52), the flood of notes in the alto spills up over the low-lying soprano.

Last beat of mm.	135	139	143	147	150
Orchestra	x	x	free x	x	x cad.
S					*c.f.* b₂
A	1	2	3		4*
T		1	2	3	
B			1		4*
Continuo	stacc. eighth note chords, followed by eighth-note rests				
Keys	g	B♭	E♭		c

* = last m. of subject 1, sequentially repeated

Though the strict triple fugato comes to a stop at the entrance of the cantus firmus, the contrapuntal excitement continues, employing among others the last measure of fugal subject 1, sequentially repeated (No. 4 on the chart) in the basses (m. 149 f.) and altos (m. 152 f.) Except for four free imitative measures between Ob. I and Vn. I (142-45), the dotted rhythm of *x* in the orchestra lends forward motion to the vocal fugato. Bach knew instinctively when he could allow his imagination to triumph over Nicolai's poise; for he did so precisely at the phrase which, in relation to the whole tune—halfway through its second part—and in relation to the words—*alleluja*—made such freedom esthetically justifiable.

With b₃, and after an interlude of *x* in C minor, Bach re-establishes the leadership of the chorale tune in the soprano (even if only by the headstart of an eighth note). The excited exhortations beneath it are reduced to the old time relation of eighths to dotted half notes. On the sustained last cantus-firmus tone, the continuous syllabic dovetailing of "macht euch/bereit" gives way, after a dramatic rest, to chordal shouts that swing the key around to the subdominant A♭ major. The exuberance generated by the tumultuous *alleluja* is still in evidence when the shouting by the altos, tenors, and basses of "prepare yourselves for the wedding," in b_4, extends well beyond the final chorale note of the sopranos (m. 174 ff.; less so in m. 165 f.). The repetition of the words "macht euch bereit," (actually the property of b_3, not of b_4), suggests an agitated return to what preceded it. In measure 171 the bass seems to look back even further. Is this one-measure flourish reminiscent of the *alleluja* fugato or does the bass try to fall in line with the follow-the-leader game that Vn. I and Ob. I are playing here? Again the restlessness during the first three cantus-firmus measures (170-72) gives way to syllabic declamatory shouts by alto, tenor, and bass, set to the text of both b_3 and b_4. By extending three measures beyond the end of the cantus-firmus phrase b_4, they overlap the customary 4-measure orchestral interlude, reducing the latter to a single measure.

The traditional supremacy of the cantus firmus, never in doubt during the two *Stollen*, is now restored by the simultaneous entrance of all voices at the last chorale phrase a_3; and this time the last cantus-firmus note of the sopranos is sustained until the other voices have completed their thrice-reiterated "You must go forth to meet him." A repeat of the orchestral ritornel rounds out this imposing opening movement, a splendid example of a chorale fantasy—which is, however, just one of 77 composed by Bach. But it is an exceptionally perfect one, in which the "unity of effect" is achieved through an unusually eloquent "diversity of detail."[19] To this belongs the basic separation of the instrumental from the vocal material, of which the instrumental represents the rhythmic and historically newer and the vocal the melodic and historically older factor of the composition. The oldest, Nicolai's tune, soars above both. In this chorale fantasy Bach succeeded in incorporating "the emotional significance of both melody and the words of a chorale in a larger structure that is at once independent of the chorale and yet forms an organic unity with it."[20] The miracle that the chorale "simultaneously stands out from the main tissue and forms one flesh and blood with it"[21] could only have been wrought by a genius whose poetic instinct and "consummate command of polyphony" enabled him to solve "these blended problems of expression and design."[22]

19. W. G. Whittaker, *Fugitive Notes on Certain Cantatas and the Motets of J. S. Bach*, London, 1924, p. 55.
20. This definition of a chorale fantasy is given by the Wagner biographer Ernest Newman in the article on Hugo Wolf (!) in Oscar Thompson's *International Cyclopedia of Music and Musicians*, New York, 1943, p. 2066.
21. *Ibid.*
22. *Ibid.*

FORM OF MOVEMENT I

	Orch. Rit.	Stollen (A)	Orch. Rit.	Stollen (A)	Orch. Rit.	Abgesang (B)	Orch. Rit.
MEASURES	16 4+4+8		16 4+4+8		12 4*+8		16 4+4+8
THEMATIC MATERIAL	x - y - z	a_1-x-a_2-y-a_3	x-y-z	a_1-x-a_2-y-a_3	y*-z	b_1-x-b_1-x***-b_2-x-b_3-x-b_4-a_3	x - y - z
TEXT LINES		1 2 3		4 5 6		7 8 9 10 11 12	
KEYS	E♭				B♭	g c A♭ E♭ B♭ E♭	

Abbreviations: Orch. Rit. Orchestral Ritornel.

*   y modulates, while z is presented literally in the dominant.

***   triple fugato on new alleluja subject. Fugal entrances: A, T, B.

Movement II

Secco Recitative

Tenor; Continuo   **C** ; C minor

Er kommt, er kommt, der Bräutgam kommt![23]	He comes, he comes, the Bridegroom comes!
Ihr Töchter Zions kommt heraus,[24]	Daughters of Zion come forth,[24]
Sein Ausgang eilet aus der Höhe[25]	he is hurrying from on high[25]
In euer Mutter Haus.[26]	into your mother's house.[26]
Der Bräutgam kommt, der einem Rehe	The Bridegroom comes, who like a roe
Und jungen Hirsche gleich[27]	and a young hart[27]
Auf denen Hügeln springt[28]	leaping upon the hills,[28]
Und euch das Mahl der Hochzeit bringt.	brings you the wedding meal.
Wacht auf, ermuntert euch!	Wake up, bestir yourselves!
Den Bräutgam zu empfangen;	to receive the Bridegroom,
Dort, sehet, kommt er hergegangen.	there, look, he comes along.

Rhyme scheme: a[29] b c b - c' d e e - d' f f
Metric scheme: a a a' b - a' b b a - b b' a'

It is customary to regard the recitative as a transition to the following musical number and deal with it as briefly as possible. This attitude
has caused the recitative to be the probably least understood among
Bach's musical forms. The presence of two different kinds of recitatives
as 2nd and 5th movements of Cantata 140—to be called 140/2 and 140/5

23. Matthew 25:6.
24. Song of Solomon 3:11.
25. Luke 1:78.
26. Song of Solomon 3:4 and 8:2.
27. *Ibid.* 2:9; 2:17 and 8:14.
28. *Ibid.* 2:8.
29. The editor deviates here from W. Neumann's *Johann Sebastian Bach—Sämtliche Kantatentexte*, Leipzig, 1956, p. 328. Neumann's line arrangement divides this
phrase into two lines for the sake of the resultant rhyme but at the cost of the
meter which then would be matched nowhere in this recitative.

from now on—gives us an opportunity to reconsider this prevailing bias.[30]

Johann Mattheson[31] speaks for the theorists of his time when he says that "the recitative constitutes a new and totally separate style which, because it proceeds for the most part without instruments . . . remains *Ex Lex* [i.e., outside the laws of music]." He continues: the recitative is "in relation to law-abiding music precisely what prose is . . . in relation to poetry." This low opinion of the recitative has to be revised in the case of Bach. Already Spitta[32] observed that:

> Bach is the only one who . . . created anew . . . . The vocal parts of his recitatives are governed by a general musical principle which hovers above the laws of declamation, with which it coincides frequently, but to which it also not infrequently runs counter, forcing them to submit to him . . . . The melodic stream in Bach's recitatives is at times so full and even, that one can abstract it confidently and totally from the words of the text.

While Spitta exaggerates, since the melody in a recitative can hardly be divorced from its text, it can be shown that a recitative by Bach is a work of art that creates and follows its own laws.

Bach takes over a great number of characteristics from the recitative style of his time. The eighth note is the unit for each syllable. The *iambic* meter with its typical upbeat is, despite the variety of Bach's text-writers, the norm. So is common time. The vocal line takes from the text its musical structure of sentences, phrases and sub-phrases. This is to say, a rounded musical sentence corresponds to each sentence of the text, complete with (usually) stereotyped cadence. Also, each text line is customarily matched by a musical phrase which, in case of exclamations and exhortations, is subdivided by short rests corresponding to the punctuation of comma, exclamation mark, etc. (see 140/2). These short fragments, however, remain integral parts of the whole musical phrase. While eighth and sixteenth rests divide and separate phrases, the quarter rest separates musical sentences.

The melodies of the *secco* recitative are naturally chosen from the chords dictated by the figured bass, which are taken apart tone by tone, so to speak, and re-assembled. Yet how infinite is the variety with which

---

30. The findings of Hermann Melchert's excellent doctoral dissertation, *Das Recitativ der Kirchenkantaten Joh. Seb. Bachs*, Frankfurt a.M., 1958, are drawn upon in our discussion of these two recitatives.

31. Johann Mattheson, *Das Beschützte Orchestre*. Quoted by Melchert, *op. cit.*, p. 144 (translated by the editor).

32. German edition, I, p. 489 (editor's translation).

Bach organizes the order and direction of these triadic tones, adds tone repetitions, passing tones, suspensions, etc., at the same time allowing the harmonically available pitch material to vibrate to the subtlest rhythmic changes that his insight into text-structure and meaning divines.

The bass usually consists of a continuous line of whole and half notes. But it tends to begin with an organ point of several measures duration and to end with cadential quarter notes. These prepare and then— frequently after a quarter rest, during which the voice has *its* cadence—mark the end of a musical and textual sentence. The stereotyped V–I chords are then sounded while the voice rests. They end, practically always, on the 1st or 3rd beat of the measure.

How do the two recitatives of Cantata 140 correspond to these essential characteristics? The first (140/2) is as pure a *secco* recitative as one is likely to encounter. It is syllabic throughout and follows the norm by using for its key the relative minor of the preceding movement and passing it on to the subsequent aria. Its three musical sentences follow those of the crudely rhymed text. The poet takes his cue from the 1st stanza of Nicolai's hymn and supplies Bach with its logical continuation. The tenor announces the arrival of the Bridegroom. The excitement betrays itself by the repetition of the words: "Er kommt" which is unusual in a recitative text. Bach dramatizes Christ's coming by the upward leap of a minor 6th, which he throws into even sharper relief by letting the voice descend down the notes of the C-minor triad on the three preceding syllables. By observing the rules of proper declamation, he gives the comma between the two exclamations its due with a sixteenth rest which, in turn, shortens the 3rd note to a sixteenth. Thereby Bach not only prevents this c^1 from becoming a premature tonic resting point but gives it springs, so to speak, to leap from the realm of c minor to the high ab^1 (of the subdominant). Since the next sub-phrase—"the Bridegroom comes!"—is uninterrupted, Bach, who knows his rhetoric, declaims it in even eighth notes. Continuing to define his key, he turns to the dominant. But instead of descending by thirds as before, Bach disarrays the order in which he presents the notes of the G-major triad by starting with the more exposed b♮ which, as diminished seventh after ab^1, heightens the tension. Finally the same upward skip of a minor sixth returns us to the tonic at the end of the first textual line and musical phrase.[33]

33. Did Brahms, enthusiastic subscriber to the *Bach Gesellschaft* edition that he was, have this opening in his subconscious mind when he began composing his Fourth Symphony? The *BG* volume containing Cantata 140 reached Brahms in 1882; the Fourth Symphony was composed in 1884/85.

In contrast to the giant steps with which Bach portrayed Christ's coming, the "daughters of Zion come forth" meekly, ascending step by diatonic step (line 2) from the lowest tone of the recitative, to which Bach relegated them. How differently "he is hurrying from on high!" In jagged leaps, including the augmented fourth, line 3 reaches the peak tone of the recitative (a♮^{1}, foreign to C minor) on the appropriate word "*Höhe*" (height). As line 4, shorter by one iambic foot than the preceding three, closes the first sentence, Bach now had to compromise with a conventional cadence. Instead of the most familiar one, ending with the drop of a fourth (see 140/5), Bach chose here the cadence with the concluding falling third:

However, the implied appoggiatura was certainly executed according to the prevailing custom (see example). As this applies also to the melodi-

cally identical second cadence (m. 9), we have in these two brief instances the only moments in which the syllabic *parlando* style yields to a hint of *cantabile*. The dramatic nature of this recitative allows the calming influence of the slur, if executed at all, only at these two resting points. In the final, almost identical cadence, the application of appoggiatura adds no slur (see example). These quasi-identical cadences unify

the ends of the three recitative sentences. At the same time they define the harmonic plateaus of the 13-measure movement by cadencing in three different keys: G minor (V), B♭ major (V of III), and C minor (I). The classic V–I chords of the continuo close each one of the three cadences.

Since the next textual and musical sentence (mm. 6-9) quotes from the *Song of Songs* the beautiful simile of "a roe and a young hart," Bach finds no reason to use the exciting leaps and sudden rests that characterized the vision of Christ's coming in the first sentence. In fact, he bathes this bucolic picture in the warm keys of E♭ and B♭ major. Although the opening phrase "The Bridegroom comes" (m. 6) is textually identical with the second half of line 1, Bach sets it now to the evenly descending tones of the G-minor triad he had avoided before, in m. 2. All but the first of the phrases comprising the second sentence begin with the same note that had ended the previous phrase. This contrasts not only with the two other sentences of this recitative but with Bach's general recitative practice. Except for two almost imperceptible sixteenth rests, Bach fuses these phrases into one 4-measure sentence. The center of the recitative is thus lyric and legato. The phrases are further unified by the use of descending triads. At the same time a sense of climax is attained by the barwise rise of peak tones from d¹ to f¹ to a♭¹ and back to f¹, and the B♭-major cadence. It is appropriate that the "young hart" should "leap" to the top note a♭¹ at the words "upon the *hills*." That the three descending triads outline the same keys, in the same order (G minor, B♭ major and C minor—though barely suggesting the latter) as the cadences of the three sentences of this recitative, is one more sign of evidence of Bach's subtle and pervasive organizing power.

The poet had tried to avoid the dactyl which occurs when two short syllables meet, by ending line 5 with the word "Rehe" (roe). Bach expressed his dissatisfaction with this separation in mid-phrase by disregarding it. He introduced a sixteenth rest at the comma (m. 6), where it rhetorically belongs, and then joined the phrase in question with the next one, composing it as a dactyl:

With the third sentence, in which he exhorts the virgins to receive the Bridegroom, the textwriter returns to the present. The ascending fifth gives the "Wake up" the immediacy of a bugle call, and Bach follows it up promptly with the fastest phrase of the recitative, the ascending and keychanging "bestir yourselves!" (m. 10). With the next phrase, dignity is restored. The even flow of eighth notes reiterates the flattened d¹ three times before letting it slide down to a♭. This phrase seems like a gesture of submission, as if the virgins were standing with their heads bowed "to receive the Bridegroom." Suddenly Bach makes them lift their eyes by crying out "dort" (there). Up an octave, to the peak tone a♭¹—not on the beat, but on the weak last eighth of the measure and followed by a quarter rest on the strong 1st beat—this shout is to shock the virgins into sudden realization of Christ's approach: "look, there he comes along." At these last words the emotions subside and the recitative ends with the familiar cadence, now in C minor.

The above may have shown to what extent a simple recitative by Bach is more than declamatory speech-song. No matter whether it be derived from prose or rhymed text, the finished product is, contrary to contemporary esthetic judgment, a subtly organized musical structure. In a Bach recitative all elements complement one another in such a way as to result in a higher unit, which is larger than the parts that compose it.

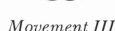

Movement III

Aria (Duet)

Violino piccolo; Continuo   Adagio;[34] 6/8; C minor
Soprano, Bass   Modified (or free) *da capo* form
Quartet texture

TEXT LINE

1	Soul:	Wann kömmst du, mein Heil?[35]	When will you come, my salvation?[35]
2	Jesus:	Ich komme, dein Teil.[36]	I am coming, your own.[36]
3	Soul:	Ich warte mit brennendem Öle.[37]	I am waiting with burning oil.[37]
4		Eröffne den Saal	Throw open the hall
5		Zum himmlischen Mahl![38]	to the heavenly banquet![38]

34. The Adagio designation is found in the original violino piccolo, continuo, and bassoon parts.

35. Isaiah 62:11.

36. "Dein Teil" (your part) makes no sense when translated literally; it makes, in fact, little enough sense in the original German, where it appears solely for the sake of the rhyme.

37. Genesis 49:18; Matthew 25:4.

38. Song of Solomon 2:4.

(4)	Jesus:	Ich öffne den Saal	I open the hall
(5)		Zum himmlischen Mahl.	to the heavenly banquet.
6	Soul:	Komm, Jesu!	Come, Jesus!
	Jesus:	Komm, liebliche Seele!	Come, lovely Soul!

Rhyme scheme: a a b c c b'
Metric scheme: a a b a a b

The two duets that hold corresponding positions in the overall *chiastic* design of the cantata are both scored for soprano, bass, continuo and one high-pitched obbligato instrument; the oboe in movement 6, the violino piccolo here. While in 140/1 the text referred to the Bridegroom and the Wise Virgins, and in 140/2 to the Daughters of Zion, here in 140/3 the Bride is identified as the Soul, the Bridegroom as Jesus. In the 4th movement the Bride is Zion.

In the seven years that lay between the publication of the 1st and 2nd volumes of his Bach biography, Spitta had come emotionally to terms with Bach's pietistic love duets. In 1873, the one in Cantata 21 had embarrassed him (see p. 111). In 1880 he calls those in Cantata 140 "duets of the highest art, which breathe of chaste fervency without ever touching on the domain of personal passion."[39] Bach certainly turned the text, a curious mixture of platitude (lines 1 and 2) and mystical rapture (lines 4-6), into a duet of sensuous beauty. He treats the longing of the Soul and the reassuring words of Christ, not in the imitative style so typical of duets, but as a true dialogue of brief question-and-answer phrases. Reiterated time and again at different tonal levels and in ever-changing variations, these fill most of the vocal portions of the movement. Not even at all cadential points—only at half of them—do the voices unite in the blissful parallel motion that is one of the joys of duet writing and singing. Bach's question-and-answer pattern has the advantage of allowing the voices to exploit the textual implications to the fullest without instrumental interference. At the same time the ritornel material keeps the wealth of vocal sentiment within reasonable boundaries by supplying a *concertante*, instrumentally conceived counterpoint to it: *e pluribus unum*.

What lifts this movement above the level of the duet in Cantata 21, and hence may have contributed to Spitta's change of mind, is the violino piccolo part. Winding in and out of the vocal dialogue, it seems to

39. Spitta, *op. cit.*, II, p. 460.

improvise its richly embellished melodic line, though it is in reality guided and firmly carried by the evenly throbbing continuo.

Schweitzer[40] draws attention to the resemblance between the *Siciliano* of the 4th Sonata for violin and harpsichord and the solo violin part of the alto aria *Erbarme dich* from the *St. Matthew Passion.* Paul Mies[41] extends this relationship logically to the violino piccolo part of 140/3. However, the profound pathos that is maintained throughout the first two compositions applies in our duet only to the first two measures. These share with the violin sonata the C minor key, 6/8 meter, and a less literal use of the dotted *Siciliano* rhythm. From the violin solo of the alto aria from the Passion, the opening motif of our duet inherited its first 4 notes with their expressive double appoggiatura. Like most German composers of the time, Bach denotes the conjunct double appoggiatura (or slide) by a *custos*-like symbol which shows that the main note is approached from the third below and on the beat (cf. score). If properly executed (see example), it anticipates the thirty-second notes that are

such a prevalent feature of the ritornel. The three related movements have further in common the use of the solo violin, or the violino piccolo.

Pirro[42] gives a very secular interpretation of Bach's choice of the small violin, viewing Christ as lover, accompanied by the instrument of students and serenaders, the dancemaster's fiddle. As mentioned earlier (p. 115), Bach is more likely to have been influenced by the instrument's association with night music (*Nachtmusiken*), which Leopold Mozart noted in 1756 and, above all, by the penetrating sound of this tuned-up violin, which in our duet has to compete with two enthusiastic voices.

All-important is that voices and solo instrument have only the opening double phrase in common (a_1 and a_2 as in mm. 1 and 2). It is used by the voices, almost as a motto, at the beginning of each section of part I (mm. 9-10 and 19-20) and of its free da capo (mm. 63-66). Except for this, the diminutive violin is on its own and develops expressive ornamentation of a richness that is wholly violinistic in nature. The brilliant curves of thirty-second and sixteenth notes, which look like the essence of

40. *Op. cit.,* I, p. 395.

41. *Die geistlichen Kantaten J. S. Bachs und der Hörer von heute,* Part II, Wiesbaden, 1960, p. 67.

42. *Bach. Sein Leben und seine Werke,* German ed. [by Bernhard Engelke], Berlin, 1922, p. 134.

the Baroque in the original part written by Krebs, are a necessary antidote to the "Affect" of the opening phrase. Bach could not have helped but associate this opening (composed in 1731) with the weeping of Peter, which precedes the solo violin part in the *St. Matthew Passion* (1729). However, since Bach composed in 140/3 not a duet of suffering and remorse but one of yearning and hope, he had to abandon the model of the Passion. In fact Bach turns the ritornel into a succession of three apparently independent motifs (see chart, p. 134). Arabesques of thirty-seconds (b), each repeated and their last 3 notes changed (b') fill measures 3 and 4 with G- and B♭-major harmonies. They culminate (in m. 5) in an impassioned phrase, rhythmically and melodically more individualistic (c). This phrase restores the minor key, F, and reaches the peak tone of the ritornel. But the subsequent chromatic descent of the two impressive pairs of sixteenth notes has the effect of sighing or pleading in vain, perhaps in anticipation of the Soul's worried question: "When will you come, my salvation?" This defeatist mood is heightened by the repeat of c a fourth lower (m. 6). Two further variants of b (b'' and b''', m. 7) lead by an upward skip of an octave to the brief C-minor cadence (*cad.*).

The opening motif, which seemed like an unbroken phrase when played by the violino piccolo, is now distributed among the two voices (a_1 and a_2) however enriched and emotionally intensified by additional single and double appoggiaturas and by the presence of the pleading figure, c, in the violin. The first vocal part of the duet is in *Bar* form. It consists of two 10-measure sections (A and A')—the 1st moving from C to G minor, the 2nd remaining in the dominant—and a 4-measure epilogue without the solo instrument (mm. 9-32). A ends with a_1, a_2 and two descending variants of a_2 in the violin (mm. 15-18). A' begins with a repeat of a_1 and a_2 in the voices, but now in the dominant and with different and new embellishment by the violin. After touching E♭ major twice (here in mm. 21-22, as in mm. 11-12 before), the soprano sings the 3rd text line: "I am waiting with burning oil," sustaining the word *"warte"* (wait) the second time for 2½ measures. At the same time the violino piccolo plays (except for its two opening measures) the whole ritornel in the dominant (mm. 23-28). Only in the last measure, and its counterpart in the da capo (m. 76), do all four parts join in one common cadence. An epilogue of four question-and-answer measures (29-32) reaffirms the G-minor key and gives the continuo, in the absence of the violin, a brief opportunity for greater freedom of movement. Half of the ritornel (consisting of a_1, a_2 $\frac{1}{2}c'$, b'' and cad.), ends part I of the duet, properly in the dominant, but played high on the upper string of the shrill diminutive violin.

The middle section (II) is not contrasted to part I but rather grows out of it. Ritornel quotations are confined to c, which serves as instrumental decoration and structural unification. Harmonically, part II moves farthest away from the tonic: to the relative major and its dominant and subdominant. Part II is composed of two *Stollen* (B and B'). Each of these is again ten measures long, based on text lines 4-6, and followed by shortened versions of the ritornel. Both vocal sections (*B* and *B'*) open with a motif (*d*) which, rhythmically identical with a_1, presents its 2nd to 4th notes by melodic inversion. In addition to this, a turn replaces the double appoggiatura of a_1 and sweeps the phrase upwards, as if to give life and space to the text "I open the hall." The sustained last note on "Saal" (hall) gives not only the feeling of a new dimension, but also functions as Christ's answer to the sustained notes which represented the "waiting" of the Soul in part I (mm. 23-26 there, vs. 37-40 in B and 51-54 in B'). This kinship between *d* and a_1 is reinforced by the similar contrapuntal background of the violino piccolo (c, c in mm. 9-10; c, $\frac{1}{2}$ c, c, $\frac{1}{2}$ c in mm. 37-40; and 4 times $\frac{1}{2}$ c in mm. 51-54). The 1st *Stollen*, B, has still to free itself of the G-minor key that preceded it before it cadences first in B♭ major (m. 42), and eventually in the relative major, E♭ (m. 46).

Again, half of the ritornel keeps the vocal parts separated. This time it consists of variants of *b*, which move up from E♭ to F and B♭ before cadencing in E♭ major. B' now is heard in clear major. After an E♭ major cadence (m. 56), there follow two measures which, except for wider skips, recall measures 11-12 of part I. Paralleling B, B' now moves from E♭ to its final cadence in A♭ major (m. 60). In this relative major of the subdominant (or vice versa), a_1 and a_2 reappear. Although no more than a token repeat of the ritornel, this suffices as an instrumental bridge that swings the music around to a free da capo, A'' (m. 63 ff.).

After a "wrong" start in F minor, the voices take up a_1 and a_2 once again, without the violin, but now in the proper key of C minor. The next measures (67-69), by their total identity with measures 13-15, confirm the view of A'' as a shortened da capo of part I.

The ritornel appears as the instrumental introduction, as the conclusion and—shortened—in several interludes of this movement. Moreover, it is its presence in all vocal sections that gives the movement its coher-

FORM OF RITORNEL (RIT.):

Mm. 1-2 $a = a_1 + a_2$
m. 3 b, b' (G major)   sequential
m. 4 b, b' repeated a third higher   (B♭ major)   sequential
m. 5 c (F minor)   sequential
m. 6 c repeated a fourth lower   sequential
m. 7 b'' sequential
     b''' a third lower
m. 8 cadence   (C minor)

SUMMARY OF OVERALL FORM OF MOVEMENT

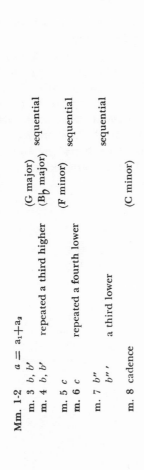
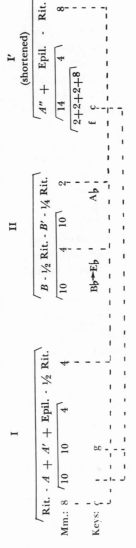

ence. In addition to the great number of ritornel quotations, substantial ritornel portions furnish the motivic violin background for the vocal sections.

In part I, the ritornel was distributed in leisurely fashion among the two vocal *Stollen* (a_1, a_2 in mm. 15-16, the rest in mm. 23-28). In the abbreviated da capo (A''), it appears as one uninterrupted block of sound in the tonic (mm. 69-76). It thus organizes, more tightly than mm. 23-28 had done before, the major portion of A''. Together with the final da capo of the instrumental ritornel, this creates a structural double frame at the end of the movement. One might further observe that in measures 71-74 the voices as well as the continuo are identical (a fifth lower) with their counterparts in part I (mm. 23-26). The 4-measure epilogue without the violin gives the voices more freedom (only the cadence—mm. 79-80—is identical with mm. 31-32, and the bass voice in m. 77 with that of m. 29). But this freedom is only ornamental, for it rests on the continuo which (in mm. 77-80) outlines its old bass (of mm. 29-32), now in the tonic. Not even the final instrumental da capo of the ritornel is completely literal, as that of the first movement had been. Here Bach leads into it with new sixteenth notes (m. 80), after which a different, more interestingly figured bass characterizes the first of its 8 measures (m. 81).

Movement IV

Nicolai: Stanza 2

Vn. I, II and Va. in unison; Continuo
Tenor (*c.f.*)

Bar form **C**; E♭ major
Trio texture; Unison Chorale

CHORALE PHRASE	TEXT LINE		
A	a_1	1	Zion hört die Wächter singen,	Zion hears the watchmen singing,
	a_2	2	Das Herz tut ihr vor Freuden springen,	for joy her very heart is springing,
	a_3	3	Sie wachet and steht eilend auf.	she wakes and rises hastily.
	a_1	4	Ihr Freund kommt vom Himmel prächtig,	From heaven comes her friend resplendent,
A	a_2	5	Von Gnaden stark, von Wahrheit mächtig,	sturdy in grace, mighty in truth,
	a_3	6	Ihr Licht wird hell, ihr Stern geht auf.	her light shines bright, her star ascends.
	b_1	7	Nun komm, du werte Kron,	Now come, you worthy crown,
B	b_1	8	Herr Jesu, Gottes Sohn,	Lord Jesus, God's own Son,
	b_2	9	Hosianna!	Hosanna!
	b_3	10	Wir folgen all	We follow all
	b_4	11	Zum Freudensaal	to the joyful hall
	a_3	12,	Und halten mit das Abendmahl.	and share in the Lord's supper.

Rhyme scheme: a a b - c c b - d d (e′) e e e

This is the only movement of the cantata that was published in Bach's lifetime. When in the last years of his life Bach collected and sifted what seemed to him most worthy of preservation, he remembered this movement, although he had probably performed it only twice before, in 1731 and 1742. Bach chose it to head the Six Organ Chorales that Schübler published in 1746 (?). This indicates a special affection for this unison chorale on Bach's part—an affection that we share today. The organ version, a strict trio, lacks the warmth of the harmonies with which the figured bass enriches the cantata movement. At the same time, Bach discovered three false relations in the original movement (in m. 18 between tenor and continuo; in m. 20 between strings and tenor; and in m. 56 in the continuo) which he corrected in his adaptation for the organ. These errors and the use of the turn in the first duet (m. 37 ff. and 51 ff.) had caused Rust to regard 1742 as the year in which Bach composed the cantata.[43]

Schweitzer[44] makes a curious observation. He calls Bach's string tune "a simple dance melody" with which "the chorale is combined dissonantly, as if it had nothing to do with it." By "dissonantly" Schweitzer must have meant a rhythmic, rather than melodic, clash between Bach's contrapuntal tune and Nicolai's chorale melody; that is, the two-dimensional effect created by the embedding of the chorale melody, phrase by phrase, into another musical organism that has its own logical but different phraseology. While Schweitzer puts his finger on the true esthetic problem of this movement, Schering[45] minimizes it in speaking of Bach's tune "as a secondary agent of counterpoint to the original melody." Yet he admits that both "are contrasted: the peaceful chorale as the eternal state with the unceasing decorative instrumental voice portraying the idea of human passion." There is hardly a Bach scholar who has escaped the particular fascination of Bach's tune. When Whittaker[46] calls the "mystic, swaying dance of the Bridesmaids ... one of the finest melodies ever created by man" he makes no profound statement. But he speaks to the point when he says "unfettered imagination could invent no more glorious tune." All writers agree that even without the chorale this would be a beautiful and complete piece of music. While everyone is affected by the tune, no one describes it adequately.

This is the only movement of the cantata to banish the violino piccolo from the string ensemble. The diminutive violin could have played along, though an octave higher (as it does in the final chorale) because the notes below b♭ exceed its compass. Instead, Bach asked the violas to

43. In this he was proven wrong. Cf. p. 51.

44. *Op. cit.*, II, p. 247 f.

45. Arnold Schering, *Foreword* to Eulenburg pocket score of *Cantata 140*, London, 1930, p. iii.

46. W. G. Whittaker, *The Cantatas of Johann Sebastian Bach*, London, 1959, I, p. 475.

join the two violins in unison and notated all three in the alto clef. There is thus no question that Bach had a rich, sonorous quality in mind for his "glorious tune." Its melody lies low and has the extraordinary compass of almost two octaves (from g to $e\flat^2$ in the initial statement). The tune is 12 measures long and consists of 5 phrases (called here: *v, w,*

x, y, and *z*). Since *x* (m. 7) is the only phrase that is just one measure long, it is heard twice. As if to compensate for this partition, *y* flows into cadential *z* without pausing for the strategically placed eighth rest that, falling on the 4th beat of measures 2, 4, 6, 7, and 8, separates· every one of the other phrases. Moreover, the disjunct principle alternates with the conjunct. If one were to reduce the disjunct nature of *v* by placing the two 2-note figures on the G string (in mm. 1 and 2) into the upper octave, one would destroy the very character of the phrase. It thrives on the little duet it plays with itself in which D and G strings are the partners. Bach apparently enjoyed this phrase enough to have it repeated as an echo (piano). Phrase *x* lives likewise on upward and downward swoops. Since it is shorter, Bach treats it sequentially. The repetition, a whole tone up, settles the previously initiated modulation in favor of B♭ major (V) by placing the decisive a♮' on the first beat. In contrast to *v* and *x, w* and *y* are conjunct and hence prefer flowing sixteenth notes to the slurred eighths that characterize particularly *v*. Just as the second of the disjunct phrases, *x*, is rhythmically less even than *v*, so is the second conjunct phrase, *y*, syncopated where the first, *w*, is not. In fact, *y* (mm. 9-10) is rhythmically identical with the 2nd phrase, *y*, of the opening chorale fantasy (see mm. 5 ff. of 140/1). After the quilt-like pattern of *v w x y*, phrase *z*, a cadential sweep of Handelian grandeur, keeps its disjunct and conjunct elements balanced. The momentum built up by *y* carries z beyond a logical first cadential point (on the 3rd beat of m. 11) to its true cadence a full measure hence. Later, in the fourth statement (out of five), Bach is content with the non-reiterative short version of z (mm. 62-63). In its original 2-measure form z holds the entire 12-measure tune in perfect balance. Balanced too are the two halves: six measures are in E♭, the other six in B♭ major. Finally noteworthy are the slurred feminine endings that give the tune a special elegance, and also foreshadow the suspensions (appoggiaturas) to come in the next two movements.

To say that this tune and Nicolai's cantus firmus are of one flesh and blood would be exaggeration. Only their first and third phrases interlock naturally. As Bach could not rearrange the order of the chorale phrases, he had to manipulate those of his own tune. In order to insert the six cantus firmus phrases of the two *Stollen*, Bach had to switch the order of *w and x*. Beyond this, he altered both upbeats of *x* and shifted its final 3-note figure in the re-statement of *x* a whole tone up (see mm. 17-20).

Nicolai's melody must be sung by the choral tenors (rather than a solo tenor), not only because of its cantus-firmus nature but also because the text says expressly: "Zion hears the watch*men* singing." Bach presents Nicolai's hymn tune essentially unadorned. Except for two natural passing tones—one in a_2, the other in the a_3 of the *Abgesang*—the melody appears slightly embellished only in two phrases of the *Stollen*. Bach enlivens the word "springen" (m. 18) modestly but characteristically (see example). He inserts a trill for additional emphasis when a_2 is

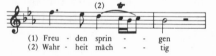

(1) Freu - den sprin - - gen
(2) Wahr - heit mäch - - tig

repeated and the word is "mächtig" (mighty). The other text passage that caught Bach's imagination is "steht eilend auf" (rises hastily) in a_3 and its repeat to the words "ihr Stern geht auf" (her star ascends; see example). Here Bach apparently intended to counteract the incongruity

(1) steht_____ ei - lend auf
(2) ihr_____ Stern geht auf

between Nicolai's descending chorale phrase and its text which both times speaks of "rising." When, on the other hand, a_3 at the end of the *Abgesang* fails to provide such textual stimulation ("and share in the Lord's supper"), Bach abstains from decorating the syllable in question

FORM OF MOVEMENT IV

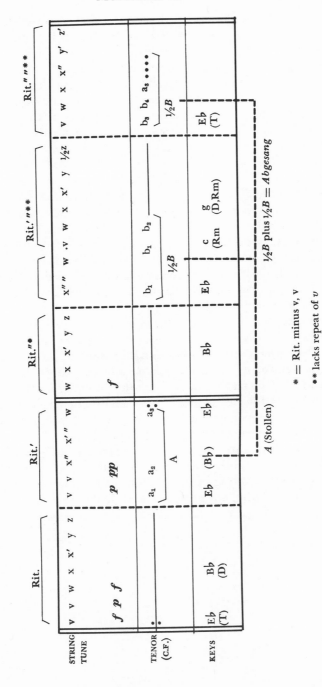

(m. 69) . In fact, all the chorale phrases of the *Abgesang* are left intact.

Bach separates the two *Stollen* by the expected literal repeat of the ritornel (one note excepted: the last in m. 27, f', which he had already so used in m. 16) . However, the ritornel that links *Stollen* and *Abgesang* omits *v*. To accommodate b_1, Bach for the fourth time alters *x*, which again precedes the unchanged *w*. Overlapping the end of the repeat of b_1 Bach begins another ritornel, which soon draws in the 4 notes of the "Hosianna," b_2. This ritornel—complete, except for the repeat of *v*—has structural as well as harmonic function: (1) it serves as an instrumental interlude separating the first three chorale phrases of the *Abgesang* from the final three; (2) it sounds the ritornel in the key of C minor, which at the proper moment (*x*, m. 58) moves to its dominant, G minor. During the final presentation of the ritornel—again complete save the repeat of *v*—and during the simultaneous interpolation of the last three chorale phrases, Bach does not have to switch the order of his contrapuntal phrases. But since the ritornel now stays in E♭ major, *x, y,* and *z* are likewise heard in the tonic. Some interesting melodic changes may be noted as they affect *y* and even cadential *z* in a way that seems calculated to cause a mild surprise.

To these two highly individual strands of melody, placed in contrast to one another, the continuo furnishes the solid harmonic foundation in tranquil quarter steps and occasional eighth-note passages. It gives the whole movement its pulse, but has no motivic individuality of its own. Harmonically, the movement is surprisingly simple. It is totally free from the sudden half-shades of minor that almost immediately clouded the harmony of the opening chorale fantasy (m. 2!), thereby preparing the listener for a movement on a vast scale and of unusual profundity. While the cantus firmus also imposes its *Bar* form on 140/4, one cannot help but feel that the subtle friction between the chorale and the periodic recurrences of the string tune and its varied phrases creates the impression, not of one form, but of a structural double exposure. (See following chart.)

Movement V

Recitative

Vn. 1 and Vn. piccolo; Vn. II; Va.; Continuo
Bass

𝄴 ; from E♭ to B♭ major

So geh herein zu mir,	Come enter in with me,
Du mir erwählte Braut!	my chosen bride!
Ich habe mich mit dir	I have pledged my troth
Von Ewigkeit vertraut![47]	to you in eternity![47]
Dich will ich auf mein Herz,	I will set you as a seal upon my heart,
Auf meinen Arm gleich wie ein Siegel setzen[48]	and as a seal upon my arm[48]
Und dein betrübtes Aug ergötzen.	and restore delight to your sorrowful eye.
Vergiss, o Seele, nun	Forget now, o soul,
Die Angst, den Schmerz,	the anguish, the pain,
Den du erdulden müssen;	which you had to suffer;
Auf meiner Linken sollst du ruhn,	on my left you shall rest,
Und meine Rechte soll dich küssen.[49]	and my right shall kiss you.[49]

Rhyme scheme: a b a b - c d d - e c f e f
Metric scheme: a a a a - a b c - a d a' c' c

Since general observations regarding Bach's recitative style have been made earlier (p. 123 ff.), the second recitative (140/5) can be discussed without preliminaries.

Its words, among them the two paraphrases from the *Song of Songs*, are those of Christ, who is traditionally represented by the bass voice and surrounded with sustained chords of all strings. The participation of the violino piccolo—unique among Bach's recitatives—makes these chords even more luminous here than usual. In spite of this "halo" around the words that Christ addresses to the Soul, the 15-measure movement is no

47. Hosea 2:19.
48. Song of Solomon 8:6.
49. *Ibid.* 2:6 and 8:3.

true *recitativo accompagnato*. It is what Werner Neumann[50] calls "ausinstrumentiertes Secco," a recitative in which the realization of the figured bass is carried out by the upper strings. These have, except for slight rhythmic shifts and natural holdovers of tones common to two chords, no life of their own. They follow the harmonic and rhythmic dictates of the continuo, from the organ points that open the musical sentences to their cadential quarter notes. Only in the penultimate measure do their emphatic quarter-note chords amount to a brief but highly effective declaration of independence (at the words "and my right shall kiss you").

Bach had to deal here with a very uneven text, again comprising three sentences. The first consists of four lines, each composed of 3 iambic feet. Its simple rhyme scheme (a b a b) gives way in the second sentence to three, and in the third to five, lines of irregular lengths and haphazard rhymes. Bach surmounts these obstacles with the ease of a master. By welding lines 3 and 4 into one phrase, he turns the vice of irregularity into a virtue, now common to all three musical sentences.

That this recitative starts in the key of the preceding movement (Eb major) is exceptional. That it modulates to the dominant, and passes this key on to the next movement, is normal procedure. In contrast to the dramatic and hence syllabic first recitative, Bach here portrays the dignity of Christ by giving most of the phrase endings the solemn emphasis of suspensions (appoggiaturas). In addition to these eight appoggiaturas, each of the three sentences has one melisma, which adds, no matter how modestly, the smoothing effect of slurred sixteenth notes. These eleven encroachments upon the syllabic style do not undermine the true substance of secco, but, aided by the full string accompaniment, they do represent a tendency towards a more cantabile style. Wide skips and rhythms, broken up by rests, produced a dramatic—in spots, even hectic—effect in the first and third sentences of 140/2. In 140/5, the choice of intervals and rests, though by no means conventional, creates, in conjunction with the appoggiaturas and melismas, an air of calm. The opening sentence of 140/5 shares with the lyrical middle sentence of 140/2 the characteristic that each phrase begins with the same note that ended the preceding phrase.

Although 140/5 is on the whole more placid, it is harmonically more adventurous than 140/2. A few examples might suffice. The I–IV–V–I

50. *Op. cit. (Handbuch . . .)*, p. 152.

scheme above the opening organ point in 140/2 is, in spite of its exclamatory rhythm, harmonically more conventional than its counterpart in 140/5. Here the curve rises after a pure E♭ major beginning, to the first melisma on d♭¹ (m. 2). While this implies the conventional seventh chord, greater harmonic depth is gained by the superimposed e♮² of the violins, i.e., by the unexpected diminished-seventh chord. Bach frequently uses the semitone mordent on the seventh degree, on the last beat of a measure and followed by a rest, to underline and give poignancy to a single word.[51] Softened here even more by the subsequent appoggiatura, it virtually caresses the "chosen bride" ("du mir *erwählte Braut*").

In the second sentence the only true expressive melisma of the movement occurs, characteristically on the word "*betrübtes* Aug" (sorrowful eye). It interrupts the even flow of eighth notes and dwells, after two sixteenth notes, on a dotted quarter note on c♭¹, top note of a chromatically altered chord: $\begin{smallmatrix}7\flat\\5\flat\\{}^{\circ}\mathrm{vii}\end{smallmatrix}$. At this point continuo and upper strings take over the throb of eighth notes. After gliding chromatically upwards from d♭ to f♮ (m. 8), the continuo passes the sudden A♭-major cadence on to the voice. This melismatic half-measure, which still lingers on in the cadential eighth notes of the upper strings above the V-I chords of the continuo (m. 9), exemplifies the way in which melody, rhythm, and harmony complement each other in the vocal and instrumental parts of a Bach recitative.

In the third sentence the continuo interprets the last reference in the cantata to past tribulations by descending chromatically (in mm. 11 and 12) to the words: "the anguish, the pain, which you had to suffer."

The first cadence (m. 4), in which the drop of a third becomes, through an appoggiatura, a diatonic descent, belongs to the type Bach used in 140/2. The other two cadences follow the most prevalent pattern, in which diatonic ascent is succeeded by the drop of a fourth. The key scheme: F minor–A♭ major–B♭ major is more unusual than that of 140/2—no matter whether we relate it to the E♭ with which 140/5 begins or to the B♭ major with which it ends. It is revealing that Bach avoids the relative minor keys of E♭ and B♭ major, respectively C minor and G minor, which were the cornerstones of the first recitative.

---

51. Henry S. Drinker, *Bach's Use of Slurs in Recitativo Secco*, privately published, n.d., p. 39.

But F minor, the subdominant strangely neglected in 140/2, is called upon as first cadence to play a vital and harmonically unexpected role in this second recitative.

Movement VI

Aria (Duet)

Oboe solo; Continuo
Soprano, Bass
Quartet texture

C ; B♭ major
da capo form

Soul:	Mein Freund ist mein!	My friend is mine!	
Jesus:	Und ich bin sein![52]	and I am thine![52]	
Both:	Die Liebe soll nichts scheiden!	Love shall separate nothing!	
Soul:	Ich will mit dir ⎫	I will with you ⎫ feed among	
	⎬ in Himmels	⎬ heaven's	
Jesus:	Du sollst mit mir ⎭ Rosen weiden,[53]	You shall with me ⎭ roses,[53]	
Both:	Da Freude die Fülle, [54] da	there fullness of joy,[54] there rapture	
	Wonne wird sein!	shall be!	

Rhyme scheme: a a b - c c b - a
Metric scheme: a a b - a a b - c (c is dactylic).

This duet is free from the complexities that characterized the first. It is in clear da capo form. Its 4-part texture is not layer put upon layer, but derived from one source: the felicitous oboe tune. In many passages this love duet thus becomes a true love trio and occasionally, when the continuo too is drawn into motivic participation, even a love quartet.

In spite of suspensions and appoggiaturas that show connection with the preceding recitative, the all-pervading principal melody is rhythmically simple, free from syncopations and transitory touches of minor keys. The solo oboe celebrates with the two voices the blissful union of Christ and the faithful Soul by sharing with them the melodic material of its 8-measure ritornel. In contrast to the many-faceted ritornel of the first

52. Song of Solomon 2:16 and 6:3.
53. *Ibid.* 4:5 and 6:3.
54. Psalm 16:11 and Isaiah 35:10.

duet, that of the second has a dance-like lilt and song-like tune. Its first two measures complement each other in happy anticipation of the use the voices will make of them time and again. The next two measures (3-4) start as if they were to repeat the initial two on the dominant. But this illusion endures for only six notes, as the true function of measures 3 and 4 is to bring the opening double phrase now into gently flowing motion. This new rhythmic buoyancy then opens the floodgates to one of those typically Baroque rolling figures of sixteenth notes (mm. 5-7) that have sequential repeats built into them. Bach lets them rise through 2½ cycles before rounding his ritornel out with an equally smoothly gliding tonic cadence.

Ritornel

MEASURES	1	2	3 - 4	5 - 7	(7) 8
PHRASE SYMBOLS	v	w	x ($= v'$ *expanded*)	y (2½ times)	z ($=$ cadence)

The next 8 measures repeat the ritornel in a most appropriate manner. Bach allows each of the voices one separate phrase (v and w), which the oboe connects with its 4-note motif, w_1, grafted from w. On the next phrase, x, Bach unites the two voices in sensuous parallel tenths, thereby translating his text literally into music: "Die Liebe soll nichts scheiden" (Love shall separate nothing). Is this what Pirro[55] had in mind when he quoted from Johann Arndt's *Four Books of True Chris-tendom* that "the first property of love is to unite the lover with the beloved thing and to transform him through it?" The one-ness into which the voices melt has been the goal of the text ever since the first duet began. Beyond symbolizing the union of two becoming one, these blissful parallel passages are also the quintessence of euphony. In addition to two added appoggiaturas (soprano, m. 12), the oboe's four sixteenth notes, w_1, provide more than tootling tokens of exuberance that link the voices now and later (mm. 16-18). They will also furnish the sole enlivening instrumental feature in the first half of the middle section

55. *L'Esthétique de Jean-Sébastien Bach*, 1907, p. 479.

(m. 47 ff.). In the next four measures (13-16) the oboe completes this first repeat of the ritornel.

With Mozartian regularity the ritornel starts out again. But this time the voices carry on beyond the literal repeat of their motto-like opening measures (17-20 = 9-12). An *arpeggio* version of *v, v″* (in the soprano; see example) is taken up by the bass a second higher, i.e. in the

canonic interval that unlike any other produces an emotional upward lift. (In reality, of course, the bass enters at the lower seventh.)

This first hint at canonic writing indicates that not even this least complex movement of the cantata will be a simple and artless piece of fluff. If part of the text suggests parallel motion, other dialogue clauses (such as "My friend is mine"—"and I am thine" or "I will with you"—"you shall with me") are open invitations to play the canonic follow-the-leader game. (In addition to mm. 21-22, canonic writing is found also in mm. 25-26, 27-28, 29-30, 35-36, 47-48, 50-52, 58-59, 64-65, and 69-72.) The next phrase (23-24), a stretto canon by inversion, does not grow out of the text but out of the composer's sheer joy of making the difficult seem simple. He even adds the opening phrase, *v*, in the oboe for good measure. Reaching text line 3 for the third time (mm. 25-26), Bach treats the inseparability of love now by close canonic dovetailing (at the tenth) in hocket style, cadencing in G minor. Above this passage, the oboe plays variants of its familiar sequences, *y*, while the continuo has incisive staccato chords. Another text repeat and more (but different) canonic imitations (at the sixth) as well as an exchange of sixteenth notes between oboe and continuo, bring the music in 8 measures around to a tonic cadence (m. 35) by way of F major. The two canonic measures that started the voices out on their own (in mm. 21-22) are now tacked on to the B♭-major close, to cadence just once more. This they do with the same delight that was to become characteristic of a classical composition fifty years later. A literal repeat of the instrumental ritornel rounds out part I.

It was at this spot that Bach took the pen from Krebs and finished writing the oboe part himself (see p. 105). In the middle section, II, Bach had to accommodate a more unwieldy text. While lines 3 and 4 rhyme with lines 1 and 2, the poet, quoting with apparent pride from Psalm 16, now attached a line in dactylic meter as coda of his iambic contribution to Cantata 140: "Da/Freude die/ Fülle, da/ Wonne wird/ sein." With sublime disregard Bach assimilated this line into the phrasing he had chosen for the duet (see m. 62 ff.). In the first half of part II the oboe plays, piano, the 4 descending notes (w_1) referred to above. After four measures they change direction at will and invite the continuo to join them in hocket fashion. Between these outer lines, the voices proceed in brief stretto canons, first at the fourth (mm. 47-48), then at the fifth (mm. 50-52). The expected modulations eventually lead, via C minor (m. 51) and G minor (mm. 56 and 59), to E♭ major. The melodic phrases are for the most part variants of v, of its arpeggio version (v''), and of w. They are interrupted, however, by increasingly longer melismas that blossom forth on the word: "in Himmels Rosen *wei*den" (*feed* among heaven's roses). Bach uses the last and longest of them (mm. 59-61) as a springboard for his climactic, homorhythmic treatment of the last text line and his enthusiastic, though structurally premature, return to major. As if the return to part I were already accomplished, the next measures (64-67) repeat, in E♭ major, measures 35-36 almost literally and 37-38 "in kind." The oboe, which had participated in these reminiscences (with y), now gets ahead of the conventional scheme by giving out a "wrong" start of the ritornel in the "wrong" key of E♭ major (mm. 67-68). Realizing that the middle section ought to close in the relative minor, Bach cuts this premature pseudo-da capo short by giving us, in the same rhythm as before, his final version of the dactylic text line. Its verse meter is hopelessly flooded by a radiant melisma on the suitable word "*Won*ne" (rapture). What sounds like singing in parallels is in reality the cantata's last canon, which is, in appropriate conformity with the text, in unison (i.e. at the octave). After this "proper" end in G minor, the whole B♭ major part I is heard now in literal da capo.

Movement VII

Nicolai: Stanza 3

S (Cantus firmus: doubled by Vn. piccolo
[an octave higher], Corno, Ob.I, Vn.I) ;
A (Ob.II, Vn.II) ;
T (Taille, Va.);
B (Continuo = Organ, Vc., Bn.)

4-part chorale harmonization
Bar form; ¢ ;E♭ major

CHORALE PHRASE		TEXT LINE		
A	a₁	1	Gloria sei dir gesungen	*Gloria* be sung to you
	a₂	2	Mit Menschen- und englischen Zungen,	with men's and angels' tongues,
	a₃	3	Mit Harfen und mit Zimbeln schon.	with harps and beautiful cymbals.
A	a₁	4	Von zwölf Perlen sind die Pforten	Of twelve pearls are the gates
	a₂	5	An deiner Stadt;[56] wir sind Konsorten	at your city;[56] we are consorts
	a₃	6	Der Engel hoch um deinen Thron.	of the angels high about your throne.
B	b₁	7	Kein Aug hat je gespürt,	No eye has ever sensed,
	b₁	8	Kein Ohr hat je gehört	no ear has ever heard
	b₂	9	Solche Freude.	such a delight.
	b₃	10	Des sind wir froh,	Of this we rejoice,
	b₄	11	Io, io,	io, io,
	a₃	12	Ewig in dulci jubilo.	forever *in dulci jubilo.*

Rhyme scheme: a a b - c c b - d d' e f f f

The three distinct manifestations in which the chorale appears in
Cantata 140 exemplify how, in a Bach cantata, the way leads from the

56. Revelation 21:21.

complex to the simple and not vice versa.[57] In the elaborate opening chorale fantasy, the cantus firmus is surrounded by two independent streams of sound: the orchestra and the accompanying voices. In the middle movement the chorale competes with a gloriously autonomous string tune, somewhat in the nature of an organ chorale prelude. In the final movement Bach gives us the unadorned chorale pure and simple. Thus three layers of sound (in 140/1) are first reduced to two (in 140/4) and now (in 140/7) to one; for in the 4-part harmonization of the chorale all voices and instruments serve the hymn tune.

Most chorales used by Bach exist not only in several harmonizations but also as separate organ chorale preludes. But of Nicolai's great tune there exists only this one harmonization (and a quite dubious chorale arrangement for organ: BWV, App. 66). This should not be surprising, since *Wachet auf* was designated as *Hauptlied* (principal hymn) for the extremely unusual 27th Sunday after Trinity. Because there was hardly any liturgical demand for this hymn, Bach used it only in this cantata. For all the unsurpassable greatness of his church music, it is a mistake to think that Bach wrote out of a craving for self-expression.

The text of Nicolai's last stanza inspired Bach to an unusually festive setting, particularly full of harmonic surprises in the *Abgesang*. The doubling of the voices by the orchestral instruments produces one unique feature. Here, although it is not necessary for technical reasons (since the soprano never descends below e♭'), Bach not only expressly asks the violino piccolo to join in with the other cantus-firmus-supporting instruments, but also to play the tune an octave higher. Its high and penetrating tones thus were intended to add a new and bright dimension of sound, which ought to be incorporated in present-day small-scale performances that aim at authenticity.

The unadorned cantus firmus notated here in half notes[58], is given a moving throb of quarter notes by the powerfully surging line of the basses. From their opening imitation (in diminution) of the first chorale notes to their simultaneous peak tones (in m. 8) and down to B♭, the basses span the interval of an eleventh. Do the twelve notes of phrase a_1 in the basses symbolize the twelve pearls that are the twelve gates of the

57. The reader is referred to the theological and general esthetic observations made in the discussion of the final chorale of Cantata 4 (Herz, *op. cit.*, p. 112 f.). Also, the acknowledgments by Bach's disciples Ziegler and Kirnberger of their master's superiority in chorale writing are as applicable here as they were there.

58. Bach customarily writes the cantus firmus in the concluding chorales of his cantatas, etc., in quarter notes.

new Jerusalem, of which the Revelation of St. John the Divine speaks and which Nicolai quotes here at the beginning of the second *Stollen*? Do these twelve notes perhaps even refer back to the midnight hour that Nicolai evoked at the identical spot in his first stanza, and that Bach may have illustrated musically by the twelve rhythmic strokes with which he opened the Cantata?

The enlivening of the slow cantus-firmus pace by quarter notes is shared in the *Abgesang* also by tenors and altos. They keep this pulsing motion flowing as unceasingly as the bass had done in the *Stollen*. The repeat of b_1 receives a movingly different harmonization from that of its first presentation. To a lesser degree this is also true of the final phrase as compared with the harmonization of a_3 in the *Stollen*. The wonder of the three C minor chords that close b_1, b_3, and b_4 is matched only by the way Bach pulls away from them in the subsequent phrases. Their asymmetrical order: c, E♭, E♭, c, c, E♭, hints at Bach's harmonic exuberance. Especially in the *Abgesang* Bach seems to summon all the powers of his harmonic genius. Here, where he is asked to express the celestial joy: ("No ear has ever heard such a delight"), his music takes wings. Skeptics who think four-part harmonization of a chorale a simple matter need only compare Bach's harmonization with the perfectly faultless and lovely one that Bach's devoted admirer and rediscoverer Mendelssohn included in his oratorio "St. Paul."

Views and Comments

CARL VON WINTERFELD †

One of the chief characteristics of Romanticism was its reaction against the progress-conscious Age of Enlightenment. The young Romantics submerged themselves in the study of the past. Protesting against the secularization of church music by the Viennese Classics, they yearned for a purer style. German Protestant musicians, sponsored by their sovereign, the music-loving King Friedrich Wilhelm IV of Prussia, pilgrimaged to Rome to find there, in the music of Palestrina and his school, their ideal of church music.

This revival of the past gave birth to the discipline of musicology, and Carl von Winterfeld (1784-1852) was one of its first spokesmen. He wrote his monumental three-volume work on the sacred song in the Protestant church towards the end of his life (1843-47). His studies in Italy had already produced a book on Palestrina (1832) and the two impressive volumes on Giovanni Gabrieli and his age (1834). They shaped his thinking as to what true church music should be, and it is by the *a cappella* ideal of the 16th century that von Winterfeld measures all church music, Bach's included.

In the second of our cantatas on the hymn and tune *Wachet auf, ruft uns die Stimme*, the relation between hymn and the insertions between its stanzas is more intimate than in the preceding cantata. Thereby [Cantata 140] has gained greater balance and inner harmony, even though the art summoned for [Cantata 80] may have been richer. * * * We know that this hymn has as its subject the entrance of the vigilant and wise virgins into the glory of the Lord, the heavenly Bridegroom. Between its stanzas the later poet has interpolated—a happy choice for the work of the com-

† In the third volume of *Der evangelische Kirchengesang und sein Verhältnis zur Kunst des Tonsatzes* (music examples, pp. 172-219), Cantata No. 140 received its first publication. It is not based on the original Leipzig parts and hence quite faulty. After his discussion of *Ein feste Burg ist unser Gott* (BWV 80), von Winterfeld turns his attention to *Wachet auf, ruft uns die Stimme* (BWV 140). The translation of von Winterfeld's remarks is by the editor and taken from pp. 330-33 of the facsimile reprint, Hildesheim, 1966.

poser—dialogues between Christ and the Soul, his Bride, relying therein on the images from the Gospel of the Day and the Song of Songs. Thus hymn and poetic insertions are vividly linked; the hymn confronts us with the present, with form and action rather than with mere contemplation and moralising. Even if the modern forms of recitatives and duets * * * are treated more warmly and tenderly, this treatment has also spread to the stanzas of the hymn. An harmonic tone hovers above the whole. If we admire the cantata based on Luther's heroic hymn [No. 80] more perhaps for its detail, this one [BWV 140] * * * will leave us with a more comforting impression.

The prelude to the first movement is solemn and majestic. Three oboes—the third of lower range than the instruments of this kind used nowadays—are grouped as a wind choir that contrasts with the three upper string instruments, while the bass forms the foundation to both. They produce the effect of a double choir, set off against one another first in the [orchestral] introduction and then in the accompaniment throughout the entire movement. They either imitate each other in ascending (or, more rarely, descending) figures or they confront the rest of the music with slurred, long-sustained sounds. The familiar beautiful chorale, assigned to the upper voices as cantus firmus, then enters simultaneously with the final note of the introduction. The three lower voices carry out an imitative web that is independent of the treble yet successfully pays attention to the meaning of each of the sung words. * * * Although the two *Stollen* * * * are set to the same music, the verbal expression appears equally appropriate in both.[1] In this fashion the first movement proceeds in dignity and splendor, elevated by the inventiveness of the Master, endowed with modesty and tenderness rather than with borrowed pomp and ornament. The subsequent recitative for the tenor leads us from the Biblical parable of the Lord to the Song of Songs. The singer summons the Daughters of Zion in the imagery of that most ancient love song: the Bridegroom is coming, appearing upon the hills like a roe and a young hart, and all should be prepared to receive him. After this summons follows the reception of Christ by the soul, in a duet for soprano and bass * * * that is accompanied only by the small violin (violino piccolo) and the bass part. * * * The violin, in a prelude hinting at the subsequent song, lets us hear the lightly skipping turns with which it later surrounds the voices. Simply from the words upon which it is based, we may surmise that in the vocal portion one voice will cut rap-

1. For a different opinion, see p. 115. [*Editor*]

idly into the other, now querying, now responding, then clinging tenderly one to the other. Both [principles] give [the duet] a suppleness and gracefulness that keep it from being fatiguing.

Now we hear the second verse of the hymn. * * * The melody is entrusted to the tenor in its original unchanged form, save for a few modest ornaments. We might not expect to hear it, for it is preceded by a totally independent two-part prelude executed by the violins and the bass. Even after the chorale has, to our surprise, entered in the midst of the prelude, the latter continues and proceeds independently until the end. It sounds like a gentle-serious wedding-dance, lovely yet dignified, and its principal motion seems to have been anticipated by the competitive play of first oboe and violin that preceded and accompanied the opening movement. The hymn tune is set off in a particularly curious way from this significant background, linked to the preceding duet as well as to the opening movement in a gratifying mutual kinship of mood.

The subsequent recitative for bass leads to a second duet of the heavenly Bridegroom and the soul. As the first duet expressed profound yearning for union, so the second now breathes the rapture of full gratification. In both, we again perceive words and images from the Song of Songs. * * * Here the oboe takes the place of the small violin as accompanist * * *; as in the earlier duet, so do we find in this intimate and warm twin-song vivid dialogue and tender blending of the voices, but the latter predominates, in conformity with its function. After this duet follows the last verse of the hymn, "Gloria sei dir gesungen," which is in four parts, without independent accompaniment of the instruments and is one of Bach's most dignified chorale movements.

In its over-all plan, as well as in the detail of its execution, this chorale cantata is doubtlessly one of the great Master's most perfect. But to what extent is the vivid expression of intimate tenderness, which is not its least ornament as an artwork and which penetrates in surprising fashion into the mood of the Song of Songs, suitable for churchly edification? The answer to this question depends on whether one can consider that part of Holy Scripture serviceable in general for churchly use. Without wishing to decide this question, we refer to the words of a worthy theologian with which he, more than a hundred years ago, introduced Melchior Frank's compositions on some parts of the Song of Songs.[2] This was perhaps the first time that the Song of Songs was granted admission into the singing of the congregation in a Protestant church.

2. D. Johannes Gerhard zu Heldburg. Cf. von Winterfeld, II, 55 f.

* * *

This cantata[3] [No. 80] seems to be endowed with unfathomably deep art; it is apparently meant to be a model of its kind. What other masters—Mattheson called them "the ancestors"—strove for in many ways of artful voice-weaving, was to manifest itself here to the highest degree, shaped to perfection by the progress of art of a later time. What the awkward gracefulness [sic] of the "dear old ones" * * * tried to accomplish with adornments, was to assert itself [here], achieved in the most perfect, most gallant splendor. But in between, the modern forms of recitative, arioso, aria, duet were to sparkle, presenting the whole as a rich bouquet of the most varied forms. And yet, if we compare this work, which is given such great preference, with the motet *Jesu, meine Freude*, which we described earlier,[4] we miss nevertheless—its splendid display notwithstanding—the profound devotion of the motet. The movements of the latter delighted us because they spoke to us through song alone [i.e., *a cappella*], and because they refrained from the variety and splendor of sound as well as from the many different forms; not to speak of the motet's magnificent contrast between hymn and Bible quotation, the foundation of the Protestant musical service, a contrast for which well-intentioned, pious, rhymed contemplation cannot compensate.

CARL HERMANN BITTER[†]

In the period of emerging musicology, those who contributed to it did not earn their living by it. Carl von Winterfeld was a high court judge, Carl Hermann Bitter (1813-85) was Prussian Minister of Finance (1879-82), appointed by Bismarck. That a Minister of Finance would write books on Bach, on Bach's sons and other musical subject matters, might give pause for comparative reflection on the cultural capacity of today's elected or appointed officials.

3. At the conclusion of his remarks on Bach's *Ein feste Burg ist unser Gott*, von Winterfeld makes this significant statement, p. 330f. [Editor]

4. III, p. 314 f. [Editor]

† From Bitter's *Johann Sebastian Bach*, 2 vols., Dresden, 1865; translated by the editor from the second edition, 4 vols., Dresden, 1880/81, I, 256 and 261.

Though the professionals Spitta and Chrysander succeeded in damaging the reputation of the "dilettante" Bitter, their abusive criticism should not have erased Bitter's contribution to music history. After Forkel's anecdotal and patriotic biography of 1802, which barely touched upon Bach's vocal music, Bitter wrote—eight years before the appearance of Spitta's first volume—the first substantial biography of Bach, and three years later, that of Bach's sons.

The cantata *Wachet auf, ruft uns die Stimme* belongs without any question among Bach's most perfect works.[1]

It can hardly be doubted that this cantata will be considered by severe critics as not properly suited for the church, in spite of the threefold appearance of the chorale, its masterful elaboration, and the way it blends into the framework of the basic Protestant text that surrounds it. The symbolic meaning of the parable of the wise virgins in relation to and in connection with the fascination of the Song of Songs and its actual implications has caused the Master to follow on his part that grave yet cheerful tone of poetic perception which the words of the text call for. Such overly severe criticism [as anticipated above] may well be answered by the conviction that the unusual perfection, greatness and purity which characterize the work under discussion, permits it to seek its place explicitly and specifically in the Protestant church, whenever and wherever she opens her doors to artistic song. Not only ascetism deserves a place there. Pious sentiment may legitimately turn also to earnest yet placid contemplations. The state of a heart, in equilibrium and in accord with God and its Savior, is not one of grief but one of joy and pious serenity.

1. Hereafter Bitter gives the complete text and a simple description of the composition. His conclusion, which appears translated above, is significant because it takes for the first time a firm stand against von Winterfeld (see above), whose bias against Bach's cantatas as true church music constituted the accepted esthetic concept of the time. [*Editor*]

PHILIPP SPITTA[†]

Spitta's (1841–94) definitive study, though in parts undermined by the recent findings of Dürr and Dadelsen, projects Bach's life and work upon the background of a whole era. Spitta's view of Bach as the Lutheran church musician *par excellence* superseded the earlier view of Bach the unexcelled contrapuntist.

* * *A hymn with its appropriate tune forms the nucleus [of 140/1], but the hymn text is not made use of for airs or recitatives, nor, on the other hand, is the hymn tune sacrificed to fanciful embellishments. On the contrary, words and compositions which, though independent, are developed out of the church hymn, are used to serve the more personal emotion which is aroused by the congregational feeling; the chorale preserves its unapproachable and unalterable nature, though it still pervades the whole as a unifying power, even where neither the original words nor the original music are to be heard.

Very closely approaching to this ideal form is the magnificent composition which Bach prepared for the twenty-seventh Sunday after Trinity of 1731, November 25. This Sunday, as is well known, but rarely occurs in the ecclesiastical year; and for this reason, and because of its poetically and mysteriously solemn Gospel, Bach felt himself prompted to compose for it a creation of the very highest order. Nicolai's three-verse hymn "Wachet auf, ruft uns die Stimme" has, with just feeling, been selected as the basis of the work; this has an obvious connection with the Gospel story of the ten virgins (*Matthew* xxv., 1–13), and it leads on and up to the beatific contemplation of the Song of Solomon and the Revelation of St. John, chap. xxi. Between the stanzas are inserted recitatives and dialogues between Christ and the Bride, duets of the highest art, which breathe of chaste fervency without ever trenching on the domain of personal passion. The three verses of the chorale are precisely at the beginning, middle, and end, and figure the mystical tone

---

† Reproduced by permission of Novello & Co., Ltd. from *Johann Sebastian Bach,* transl. Clara Bell and J. A. Fuller-Maitland, London, 1889 (New York: Dover Publications, 1951), II, 459-60.

that pervades the whole work, and which is required by the ideas of the solemn silence of the night when the Heavenly Bridegroom is looked for, and the unspeakable joys of the glory of the New Jerusalem. The first verse is a chorale fantasia; [motif y, see p. 117 above], which comes in on the fifth bar, infuses a feeling of mysterious bliss into the majestic rhythm of the orchestra, and this feeling overflows again and again in happy and expressive passages. The soprano has the melody, while its dramatic purport is indicated by the other voices in figures of wonderful significance. In the second verse, which is a trio for tenor voice, violins, and bass, the mystical sentiment is most fully brought out. It is like the dance of souls in bliss, swaying to and fro with a strange and mysterious expression on the low notes of all the violins—all Zion and the faithful have passed with Christ into the joys of the heavenly banquet. The last verse, in which "Glory, with tongues of Men and Angels"—is sung, appears in unadorned simplicity. The splendid melody has here once more an opportunity of producing its effect by its own beauty.

ALBERT SCHWEITZER†

The title of Schweitzer's Bach biography, first published in French in 1905: *Jean-Seb. Bach, le musicien-poète,* indicates that the author's chief intention was to reveal the relationship between word and tone in Bach's music. In contrast to Spitta's approach, Schweitzer's is wholly esthetic. Spitta was a historian influenced by Brahms and his concept of pure music. Schweitzer (1875-1965), under the spell of Wagner, particularly of Tristan, introduced Bach as a poet and painter in sound who, Schweitzer believed, applied the technique of the *leitmotiv* long before Wagner.

If the majority of these chorale cantatas do not make an effective whole, the fault lies in the texts, which consist of a string of strophes without any inner dramatic coherence, and without sufficient musical distinction between them. Moreover there are too many strophes in most of the cho-

† From Albert Schweitzer, *J. S. Bach,* transl. Ernest Newman (from the German edition of 1908), New York, II, 245, 247, 398, 248; reprinted by permission of A. & C. Black, Ltd., London, and the Macmillan Company, New York. Music examples have been omitted.

rales. Cantatas worked out on these chorale lines require short hymns, in which every verse suggests a different musical characterisation. These ideal chorales are very few in number. When, however, Bach finds a text of this order, we get a dramatic art-work of the most perfect kind imaginable, as in the cantatas *Ein' feste Burg* and *Wachet auf, ruft uns die Stimme.*

* * *

The cantata *Wachet auf, ruft uns die Stimme* (No. 140) deals with the parable of the ten virgins,—the Gospel for the twenty-seventh Sunday after Trinity. This Sunday comes into the church year only when Easter falls very early; as a rule there are only twenty-six Sundays after Trinity.

The first chorus depicts the awakening. All is animation; the bridegroom comes; the virgins start up in dismay from their slumber, one raising the other. In this chorus we can see very clearly the changes that have come over our conception of Bach's music. Julius Stockhausen, of Frankfort, used to bring in the orchestra *pianissimo* and work it up through a slow *crescendo*, as if distant noises were gradually coming nearer. Siegfried Ochs begins *forte* and with a very quick tempo, so as to suggest the sudden confusion caused by the "Wachet auf!" ("Awake!"). This is certainly the right way. To get the proper effect, the syncopated notes in the mounting semiquaver passages should be thrown into high relief. There need be hardly any fear of overdoing it; the more vehement the accents, the more clearly will the hearer apprehend the meaning of the motive.[1]

The second verse, "Zion hört die Wächter singen," is dominated by a simple dance melody. With this the chorale melody is combined dissonantly, as if it had nothing to do with it;[2] the cry of the watchmen strikes into the music of the procession that is drawing nigh with the bridegroom. In order that this may have its proper rural quality, it is written for the strings *unisono*, with an accompaniment in the contrabasses.

The procession arrives. In the festive hall the "Gloria sei dir gesun-

1. Later (II, p. 398) Schweitzer puts it this way: "The effects that can be made by the appropriate accentuation of even small melodic lines may be seen in the first chorus of *Wachet auf*, by accenting according to its real nature the semiquaver motive that depicts the hurried wakening, instead of according to the normal ¾ scheme." [*Editor*]

2. Cf. above, p. 136. [*Editor*]

gen" is sung. The foolish virgins are left outside in the night, in despair. Not until Berlioz shall we meet with any dramatic-pictorial music comparable to this.[3]

ANDRÉ PIRRO[†]

~~~~~~~~~~~~~~~

Pirro (1869–1943) was Romain Rolland's successor at the Sorbonne. His biography of Bach, published in 1906, and his still untranslated *L'Esthétique de Jean-Sébastien Bach* of 1907 were, like Schweitzer's book, written by a practicing musician (an organist) who was influenced by the then prevailing "hermeneutic" trend, which interpreted music in terms of its content.

In general, it is in the opening chorus of the cantata that, following a custom to which he is nearly always faithful, Bach displays his full power. In the introduction he reveals the entire content of the chorale, sets in motion both the materials the theme furnishes this architect of sounds and the ideas the text can suggest to the "musician-poet." Moreover, one must admit that very often it is only in this first strophe that the words are worthy of Bach's commentary. If, in fact, in these cantatas we exclude the last chorus where one usually finds a mere harmonization of the four-part chorale—a harmonization of genius, admittedly, but in which all musical development is forbidden—in many cases only the first strophe of the hymn subsists in its original form. The other parts of the work are composed on wretched verses by Picander, who to amplify, rejuvenate and adjust them to the cut of the Italian air, dulls the most beautiful thoughts which the author of the hymn had expressed with noble solemnity.

* * *

In the cantata *Wachet auf, ruft uns die Stimme* Bach reveals his utter devotion to the chorale. On occasions he has treated the hymn as though

3. This is the characteristic hermeneutic view of the Schweitzer/Thomas Mann generation. [*Editor*]

† From *J. S. Bach*, transl. Mervyn Savill, New York, 1957, pp. 146, 148-51, by kind permission of Grossman Publishers, Inc.

it were a sacred and inexhaustible fund, in an attempt to translate into his works the strange efficacy of this music which, thanks to long devotion, has become both intelligible and pious; he has exploited the virtue of a well-known tune and borrowed from its power of religious evocation. Here Bach no longer asks favors from the chorale; he uses it. * * * The hymn is complete: the text and the melody remain intact. When words have been added to fulfill the musical demands they are at least from Nicolai's text; they do not conflict but complete and respect the poem, just as the motifs embellish and develop it.

* * * The first chorus is preceded by a short instrumental prelude in which the violin and the oboes reply to each other. They alternate bar by bar on chords repeated to a uniform and majestic rhythm in which, however, a vague sense of emotion has begun to quiver. At the fifth bar, the violins rise above these trembling harmonies, announcing the chorale theme in a vigorous and fervent motif. The oboes resume and accentuate this noble phrase. Then everything springs to life; close-set scales suddenly rise, progress and become bathed in a light which makes them flame like sunbeams. After a resolute instrumental cadence the soprano sings the chorale. The vivid skill of the vocal parts joins with the urgent rhythms and the *ritardando* effusions of the orchestra to accompany the proud melody. Through their medium surge the images suggested by the text and the feelings it evokes. In the midst of the great descriptive outburst of the instruments and below the high line of the chorale they are plastic and lyrical. As a person exalted by the words he hears and repeats, the chorus trembles. At each verse he is a prey to the agitation the poet has unleashed in him; alternately he commands, acclaims, questions and repeats the cries of the watchmen who, from their tall towers, sound the alarm in the night. Toward the end he breaks into brilliant coloraturas of jubilation and bears even the orchestra away in a tumult of joy.

Like a herald, the tenor proclaims the arrival of the bridegroom. In a colloquy of exquisite beauty, Bach writes the dialogue of the wise virgin and the awaited fiancé, Jesus and the faithful soul. This poem is an astonishing mixture of pure desire and chaste tenderness. The voices express merely the sweetness of this love fraught with prayer and compassion. The violin accompanies them. At the outset it speaks in their voice but proceeds to relate what they cannot possibly express. In its passionate song—a whirlwind host of unutterable feelings—palpitates the mystic intoxication of the characters and the fever of their avid languor.

In the chorale variations which follow, Bach evokes the march of the elect to the festive hall to which Jesus has summoned them. After an affectionate bass recitative the final duo returns to the scene between the Saviour and the chosen soul. This duo, impregnated with bliss, has not the depth of the preceding dialogue, but although it lacks poignancy, it charms by its elegance and radiance. The cantata ends with the third strophe of the chorale sung by four voices.

C. HUBERT H. PARRY †

Through his teacher, the son of Samuel Wesley, Sir Charles Hubert Hastings Parry (1848–1918) was still connected with the English Bach revival of the early 19th century. A prodigy as composer, pianist and organist, Parry grew into a renowned composer of choral music. He was one of those musicians towards the end of the 19th century who devoted their lives to the regeneration of native English music. Parry was a born leader and true humanist, who distinguished himself also as a lecturer and scholar (cf. *The Music of the Seventeenth Century*, Vol. 3 of the original *Oxford History of Music*). He received honorary Mus. D. degrees from both Oxford and Cambridge, and succeeded Sir George Grove as Director of the Royal College of Music. Parry's pacifistic convictions and noble idealism were shattered by World War I, which hastened his death in 1918.

Parry belonged to the triumvirate of highly cultured writers and polished stylists who, in the wake of the completed *Bach Gesellschaft* edition and in the incredibly short span of five years, gave to the world the imposing pictures of the poet-musician J. S. Bach (Schweitzer, 1905 and 1908), of the esthetics of Bach's art work (Pirro, 1906 and 1907) and of "The development of a great personality" (Parry, 1909). To Parry belongs the honor of having written the first substantial Bach biography in English. The hermeneutic bias of the time is less prominent in Parry's biography than in those by his younger French and German colleagues.

After the initial chorus the solo voices come into requisition, and arias alternate with recitatives, and occasionally with movements of more Teutonic type, till the necessary measure of music for the church cantata in the service (somewhere said to be about thirty-five minutes) is completed; and then the whole is rounded off by the singing of the chorale

† From *Johann Sebastian Bach*, New York and London, 1909, pp. 386-89; reprinted by kind permission of the publisher, G. P. Putnam's Sons.

in its simple direct form, the voices in characteristic four-part harmony being usually only doubled by the instruments. This ending with the simple chorale sung once through is obviously another specialty of the Reformed service; as, apart from intrinsic qualities of an impressive kind, so short and undeveloped a movement would not appear sufficiently spacious to serve as the conclusion of a large work for chorus, soli, and orchestra. It was the deep-seated veneration for the chorale and its devotional associations which gave it significance enough to serve such a purpose. * * * While those who are ignorant of the conditions for which these cantatas were composed would be puzzled at the apparent inadequacy of the finale, those who are more happily placed can, with the help of a little experience, so transfer themselves in imagination to the situation which Bach had in his mind, as to feel through the exercise of developed artistic perception almost the full meaning of the concluding chorale and its adequacy as an element of design.

Of the two types of cantata, those which begin with the instrumental introduction and alternate phrases of the chorale with episodes, and those which begin with a chorus on the lines of the Pachelbel Choralvorspiel, it so happens opportunely that two of the finest cantatas written by Bach in the latter part of his life are remarkable examples. Of the first order is the cantata *Wachet auf* which belongs to the very outset of the period under consideration, as there seems sufficient reason to believe that it was written for the twenty-seventh Sunday after Trinity in 1731. The occasion does not seem to have been of sufficient importance to account for the exceptional splendour of the work, as it cannot be supposed that the mere fact that Sundays after Trinity do not often run to such a number could have been in the least inspiring. The source of the exceptional warmth and beauty of the work is more likely to have been that the poem was congenial and suggestive, that the subject of the Bridegroom and the Virgins appealed to Bach's imagination in the symbolical sense of its application to humanity at large, and that the chorale tune itself was exceptionally impressive.

* * * The passage which serves for instrumental introduction [to the first chorus] is rather shorter than usual, as though Bach wished to come to the point at once; but it is sufficiently long to establish the type of musical figures and the strenuous mood. * * * The rhythmic element is manifested in a march-like character produced by the energetic trochees combined with the three stern beats of the molossus. The secondary voices on the other hand are almost unrhythmic; having passages with

cross-rhythms, syncopations, overlapping melodic figures, and all such effects as suggest the individuality of the human creatures singing the various parts, at once independent and bound together by the unities of the art-work as a whole. The twofold scheme of the instrumental and vocal factors completes the scope of musical expression, the rhythmic and the melodic; the former representing the extra-ecclesiastical factors which had not presented themselves in church music before the Reformation, and the latter the primitive types of sacred music as transformed by being filtered through organ music. And over and above all the astonishing profusion of devices most perfectly assimilated the chorale soars in its long-drawn simplicity, as though undistracted by the hurly-burly of the other voices and the vivacity of the instrumental accompaniment. Yet its quasi-aloofness does not suggest indifference, but something above the rest—noble and tranquil, savouring of divine steadfastness.

* * * Bach probably felt the drawback of the form, in which the constant stopping and recommencement of the voices seriously hampers the development of climaxes; but he makes up for it by the realistic suggestion of the subordinate voices shouting, "Wohl auf, wohl auf! der Bräut'gam kommt wohl auf!" "Steht auf, die Lampen nehmt, steht auf!" in short incisive phrases, as though suggesting of a verity the ardent elation of actual human beings in the realisation of the coming of the Lord; and by introducing a brilliant fugal "Alleluia," which disguises and bridges over the gap between two of the chorale phrases.

The enumeration of the various factors of artistic form and method might be pursued indefinitely. They all combine and assimilate in his hands to interpret that highly composite human phenomenon, religious devotionalism, as affected by association, tradition, imagery, sensibility, and mystery, directed in this case with deep poetic insight to the imposing conception of mankind stirred at the immediate advent of the Lord.

W. G. WHITTAKER†

William Gillies Whittaker (1876–1944), conductor of the famous Newcastle-on-Tyne Bach Choir, made Bach's cantatas known in England; he was, indeed, the first musician to perform Bach's complete cantata output in public. The reader is also referred to Whittaker's *The Cantatas of Johann Sebastian Bach, Sacred and Secular*, London, 1959, I, 472–79. At Whittaker's death this comprehensive work was left in a state of a first typed draft. For this and other reasons, the editor has chosen to quote instead from Whittaker's earlier, far more detailed and finished *Fugitive Notes*.

It is difficult to speak of this composition without seeming to be guilty of the vice of exaggeration, yet the wonder of it all grows so much with prolonged acquaintance that there seems to be no finality to its suggestiveness and its beauty. Whether one considers the amazing opening chorus, the inimitable charm of the two duets, the magical treatment of the second verse of the chorale, the splendid harmonisation of the third, or the general balance and finish of the whole work, one feels that here the highest art, the deepest feeling, and the most exalted religious ecstasy are united into a single expression.

The general plan of the cantata is admirable; Philipp Nicolai's fine hymn is used in its entirety, the first and last verses opening and closing, and the second occupying the central position of the work. After the rousing call to awaken, a single voice speaks of the coming of the Bridegroom. The Saviour invites the Church to come to her bridal, and the second verse of the hymn describes the scene of their meeting. The Bridegroom comforts the Bride, promises eternal bliss, freedom from the tears and pains of the past. After a rapturous expression of trust and faith, the final hymn of praise is sung within the gates of the new Jerusalem.

The mystic poem was the result of a deep emotional impression

---

† Permission to reprint substantial excerpts from pp. 51-63 of W. G.Whittaker's *Fugitive Notes on Certain Cantatas and the Motets of J. S. Bach*, London, Oxford University Press, 1924, has been granted by the publisher.

produced upon Nicolai in 1599, when his spiritual flock perished by plague as corn mown down by a reaper. The splendid tune with which it is always associated is also said to be by the poet; possibly, as is the case with so many of the chorales, it may be an adaptation of some previously known melody or melodies.

Bach's imagination was brought to a white heat by the imagery of the parable of the wise and the foolish virgins, by the vision of the City of Jerusalem aroused in the dead of night with the sudden and enthralling announcement of the coming of the Heavenly Bridegroom, of the mingled confusion, alarm, despair, and joy which would follow such an awakening. The orchestra quivers with animation; nothing more vivid has been written by any later composer. * * *

Wherever in the orchestra ♩. ♪ occurs, it should be played ♪ 𝄽 ♪ . The effect is immensely more vigorous and arresting, and is quite in keeping with the rest of the instrumental portion. In fact, played as it stands it is rather tame and unconvincing. * * * The three lower vocal parts should be sung in a very declamatory manner throughout. Wherever an accent contrary to the normal occurs, it should be strongly marked, so as to create the effect of cries heard from all directions. Each part should go its own path, emphasising, phrasing, and breathing independently. * * *

To what an extent has the older form of choral prelude developed in this great chorus! * * * In the opening he shows the instrumental side; the quivering, answering chords and the rushing scale-passages are types of expression that no voices could have given us. We almost feel at first that the picture is complete. But the chorus is reserved for an equally great mission. The successive rising to the extreme notes of the men's voices, the short sharp cries of 'Wachet auf!' 'Wo, wo' are choral effects purely, and unattainable instrumentally. The vocal phrases spring only rarely here from the lines of the chorale, but are natural, declamatory counterparts of the words. The combination of these diverse elements—the vivid orchestral mass, the energetic dramatic polyphony of the voices, and the strong majestic tune—results in one of the most amazing conceptions in art.

* * *

The two duets are dialogues between the Saviour and the Church, the former given to a bass voice, the latter impersonated by a soprano. The two sing and converse almost like a pair of earthly lovers. It is a charm-

ingly naive and innocent expression of spiritual longing, which was more
suitable for Bach's day than our own, and needs the utmost care and rev-
erential treatment with modern audiences or congregations. But such
symbolism was quite customary in the Church music at the
time. * * * The first dialogue is of the most exalted beauty, every phrase
is absolutely haunting. The exquisitely tender voice parts are accompanied by a solo violino piccolo, which weaves arabesques of inimitable
charm as if twining graceful tendrils round the Bridegroom and Bride to
unite them. * * *

    * * * We cannot accept comfortably nowadays much of the reli-
gious imagery of that period. One must remember that the position of the
singers, in a gallery practically out of sight of the congregation, and the
allocation of the soprano part to a boy would make the duet more imper-
sonal and symbolical in character than we can present it in a concert-
room. In the phrases sung to the sentence just quoted, the word 'Saal'
('hall') is set to long firm notes. One can almost see the image of the
Saviour throwing open the chamber, and standing at its portals inviting
the Bride to enter.

                              *   *   *

    [In the fourth movement] the melody is given to all the violins and
violas in unison, the violino piccolo being absent, as its bright tone
would interfere with the rich sonority demanded. In performance the
chords added above the bass must be very full to balance the massed
strings.

    The address of the Saviour to the Church in the following recitative
is accompanied by strings, to give a necessary differentiation from the
narrative recitative which occurs earlier. We are reminded of the treatment of Christ's utterances in the Matthew Passion. * * *

    The captivating charm and buoyancy of spirit of the next [i.e., the
sixth] number remind us of Schubert in his gayest moods. The voices
follow one another at short distance with winning, caressing phrases, trip
along in genial thirds, or execute long florid passages where the text
speaks of 'pasturing' (or 'grazing') among Heaven's roses. All the while a
solo oboe twines its way through the soprano and bass parts like a merry
stream trickling through flower-bedecked meadows, appearing and disap-
pearing in its bending course. * * *

    The number bears the double title 'Arie (duet),' which is apparently
contradictory, but it is a common one with Bach, he even uses 'Arie

(Terzet).' The first of the two words merely indicates the form in which the duet or trio is cast. * * *

The cantata ends with the chorale in its unadorned form, harmonised in a simple and direct way quite unusual with Bach. Such treatment was the result of the unconscious sense of the fitness of things which produced masterly strokes of genius without effort. Certainly no more imposing finish can be conceived. It rounds off the work as a perfect whole and leaves the hearer with the impression that nothing more conclusive and satisfying could have been said.

FRIEDRICH SMEND [†]

Descendant of an old and renowned family of theologians, Friedrich Smend (b. 1893) is today the staunchest defender of Spitta's view of Bach as orthodox Lutheran. In his position as professor of hymnology and liturgy at the Kirchliche Hochschule in West Berlin, a post he held until 1958, Smend not only defied all attacks on this (principally correct) concept but also rejected the evidence upon which the new tradition-shattering chronology of Bach's works is based. Smend further applied to Bach's music—perhaps somewhat too generously—the symbolism, particularly the number symbolism, of 17th century Lutheran theology.

It is one of the characteristics of Pietist poetry that in it the Song of Solomon increasingly takes the place that the Book of Psalms had occupied in the hymn of the Reformation and thereafter. Simultaneous with this change—one sees in it a phenomenon of decay—the relationship of Bridegroom and Bride experiences a new interpretation. It is no longer understood as a picture of the union of God with his people, of Christ with the Church, but as a reflection of the relation between Jesus and the pious individual soul. * * * Our cantata belongs to the few works by Bach in which a Pietistic strain can be traced.

[†] From *Johann Sebastian Bach: Kirchen-Kantaten*, Berlin: Christlicher Zeitschriftenverlag, 3rd ed., 1966, Heft IV, *Ende des Kirchenjahres* [end of the church year]. By kind permission of the publisher. Excerpts from pp. 41 and 42, translated by the editor.

But not even here does Bach abandon himself to Pietism; on the contrary. Only the connecting links between the main pillars of the monumental structure show Pietistic influence. The three stanzas of Nicolai's mighty watchmen's song form the beginning, center, and end of the work. In them (and thus also in Bach's setting) the Church *as Church* comes into view with a greatness that was not in the power of Pietism to express.

KARL GEIRINGER †

Karl Geiringer (b. 1899), formerly curator of the collections of the Society of the Friends of Music in Vienna and professor of music at Boston University, taught at the University of California, Santa Barbara, from 1962 to 1971. He is also the author of biographies of Haydn and Brahms, of books on musical instruments and on the Bach family, and compiler of an anthology of music by members of that illustrious clan.

No. 140, *Wachet auf* (Sleepers wake), was written in 1731. Nicolai's beautiful hymn on which it is based deals with the parable of the wise and foolish virgins, and turns later to a description of heavenly Zion. In the first movement the chorale melody is presented in long notes by the soprano, under which the lower voices weave a vivid contrapuntal texture inspired by the words rather than by the hymn's melody. The orchestra adds a completely independent accompaniment picturing the approach of the heavenly bridegroom and the eager anticipation of the maidens. Out of these various elements grows a sound combination of overwhelming sensuous beauty. In the magnificent second chorale arrangement (No. 4) the hymn tune intoned by the tenors is joined by a completely different violin melody of a caressing sweetness rarely to be found in Bach's cantatas; this depicts the graceful procession of the maidens going out to meet Jesus, the heavenly bridegroom. In the duets preceding and following this chorale arrangement the hymn tune is not used, and the pledges that Christ and the soul exchange sound not very

† From *Johann Sebastian Bach: The Culmination of an Era*, New York, 1966, p. 175. Copyright 1966 by Oxford University Press, Inc.; reprinted by permission.

different from those of earthly lovers. The first achieves a mood of sweet poignancy with the help of the bright cantilena intoned by a violino piccolo * * * . The second, with its similarity of motives in both voices, points far into the future, to the duets between husband and wife in Haydn's *Creation* and Beethoven's *Fidelio*.

Bibliography

MUSIC

Johann Sebastian Bachs Werke, Bach-Gesellschaft edition *(BG),* 46 vols., Leipzig, 1851-1899.
Johann Sebastian Bach. Neue Ausgabe Sämtlicher Werke, Neue Bach Ausgabe *(NBA),* Kassel and Leipzig, 1954 ff.; including Critical Commentaries *(Kritische Berichte)* to each volume.

GENERAL STUDIES

In English:

Blume, Friedrich, *Two Centuries of Bach,* London, 1950.
————*Outlines of a New Picture of Bach,* in *Music and Letters,* XLIV (1963), 214-27.
————*Bach in the Romantic Era,* in *The Musical Quarterly,* L (1964), 290-306.
Bukofzer, Manfred, *Music in the Baroque Era,* New York, 1947.
David, Hans T. and Arthur Mendel, *The Bach Reader,* rev. ed., New York, 1966. This "Life of Johann Sebastian Bach in Letters and Documents" reprints in English translations the first two Bach biographies: C. P. E. Bach's and J. F. Agricola's Obituary of 1754 (pp. 213-24) and J. N. Forkel's book of 1802 (pp. 293-356).
Geiringer, Karl and Irene, *Johann Sebastian Bach: The Culmination of an Era,* New York, 1966.
Gurlitt, Wilibald, *Johann Sebastian Bach,* St. Louis, 1957.
Herz, Gerhard, *Toward a New Image of Bach,* in *Bach (The Quarterly Journal of the Riemenschneider Bach Institute, Berea, Ohio),* I/4 (Oct. 1970), 9-27.
Hindemith, Paul, *Johann Sebastian Bach: Heritage and Obligation,* New Haven, 1952.
Mendel, Arthur, *Recent Developments in Bach Chronology,* in *The Musical Quarterly,* XLVI (1960), 283-300.

Parry, C. Hubert H., *Johann Sebastian Bach: The Story of the Development of a Great Personality*, New York, 1909.

Pirro, André, *J. S. Bach*, New York, 1957 (translated from the French edition of 1906).

Schweitzer, Albert, *J. S. Bach*, 2 vols., New York, 1962 (reprinted from the English edition of 1911).

Spitta, Philipp, *Johann Sebastian Bach*, 3 vols., New York [and London], 1951 (reprinted from the English edition of 1889).
This translation should be used with care, since it is not entirely reliable.

Terry, Charles Sanford, *Bach: A Biography*, 2nd ed., London, 1933.

———*Bach's Orchestra*, London, 1932.

In German:

Bach-Jahrbuch, Leipzig, 1904 to present (after 1953, published in Berlin).

Johann Sebastian Bach in Thüringen, Weimar, 1950.

Blume, Friedrich, *Geschichte der evangelischen Kirchenmusik*, 2nd ed., Kassel, 1965.

Dadelsen, Georg von, *Beiträge zur Chronologie der Werke Johann Sebastian Bachs (Tübinger Bach-Studien, 4/5)*, Trossingen, 1958.

———*Bach-Probleme*, in *Report of the Eighth Congress of the International Musicological Society, New York, 1961*, I, 236-49.

Dürr, Alfred, *Zur Chronologie der Leipziger Vokalwerke J. S. Bachs*, in *Bach-Jahrbuch*, XLIV (1957), 5-162.

———*Zum Wandel des Bach-Bildes*, in *Musik und Kirche*, XXXII (1962), 145-52.
A reply to Blume's 1963 article listed above (which was published originally in German in 1962); pages 153-56 contain a further answer by Blume.

Geck, Martin (ed.), *Bach-Interpretationen*, Göttingen, 1969.

Neumann, Werner, *Johann Sebastian Bach. Sämtliche Kantatentexte*, Leipzig, 1956.

Schering, Arnold, *Johann Sebastian Bach und das Musikleben Leipzigs im 18. Jahrhundert (Musikgeschichte Leipzigs, vol. III)*, Leipzig, 1941.

Schmieder, Wolfgang, *Thematisch-systematisches Verzeichnis der Werke Johann Sebastian Bachs*, Leipzig, 1950 (3rd ed., 1961).

Smend, Friedrich, *Bach in Köthen*, Berlin, 1951.

Winterfeld, Carl von, *Der evangelische Kirchengesang und sein Verhältnis zur Kunst des Tonsatzes*, 3 vols., *Leipzig*, 1843-1847. Reprint, Hildesheim, 1966.

Wolff, Christoph, *Der Stile Antico in der Musik Johann Sebastian Bachs: Studien zu Bachs Spätwerk*, Supplement (*Beiheft*) to *Archiv für Musikwissenschaft*, vol. VI, Wiesbaden, 1968.

Zander, Ferdinand, *Die Dichter der Kantatentexte Johann Sebastian Bachs*, Köln, 1967.

In French:

Pirro, André, *L'Esthétique de Jean-Sébastien Bach*, Paris, 1907.

SPECIAL STUDIES

In English:

Dürr, Alfred, *Notes* accompanying various recordings of Bach cantatas released under the *Cantate* label, Kassel.

Emery, Walter, *Bach's Ornaments*, London, 1953.

Herz, Gerhard, *BWV 131—Bach's First Cantata*, in *Studies in Eighteenth-Century Music*, London, 1971, pp. 272-91.

Mendel, Arthur, *On the Pitches in Use in Bach's Time*, in *The Musical Quarterly*, XLI (1955), 332-54 and 466-80.

Schering, Arnold, *Forewords* to Eulenburg pocket scores of various Bach cantatas.

Terry, Charles Sanford, *Bach's Chorals*, 3 vols., London, 1915-21.

————*Joh. Seb. Bach. Cantata Texts, Sacred and Secular (With a Reconstruction of the Leipzig Liturgy of his Period)*, London, 1926; reprinted 1964.

Whittaker, W. G., *Fugitive Notes on Certain Cantatas and the Motets of J. S. Bach*, London, 1924.

————*The Cantatas of Johann Sebastian Bach: Sacred and Secular*, 2 vols., London, 1959.

In German:

Dürr, Alfred, *Studien über die frühen Kantaten J. S. Bachs*, Leipzig, 1951.

Melchert, Hermann, *Das Recitativ der Kirchenkantaten Joh. Seb. Bachs*, Frankfurt a.M., 1958.

Mies, Paul, *Die geistlichen Kantaten Johann Sebastian Bachs und der Hörer von heute*, 3 pamphlets, Wiesbaden, 1959-64.

————*Die weltlichen Kantaten Johann Sebastian Bachs und der Hörer von heute*, Wiesbaden, 1967.

Neumann, Werner, *Handbuch der Kantaten Johann Sebastian Bachs*, 3rd ed., Leipzig, 1967.

Schering, Arnold, *Uber Kantaten Johann Sebastian Bachs*, Leipzig, 1942 and 1950.

Smend, Friedrich, *Johann Sebastian Bach. Kirchen-Kantaten*, Berlin, 1947-49; 3rd ed., 1966.

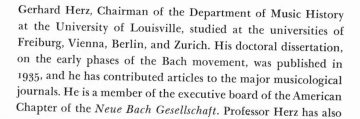

Gerhard Herz, Chairman of the Department of Music History at the University of Louisville, studied at the universities of Freiburg, Vienna, Berlin, and Zurich. His doctoral dissertation, on the early phases of the Bach movement, was published in 1935, and he has contributed articles to the major musicological journals. He is a member of the executive board of the American Chapter of the *Neue Bach Gesellschaft*. Professor Herz has also taught at Indiana University and the University of Chicago.